WAKE UP, JOHN!
...THIS IS VOLUME TWO
OF THE BICKERSONS
SCRIPTS!

VOLUME 2

The Bickersons Scripts

...JUST
TURN THE VOLUME
DOWN, BLANCHE!
...AND LET ME
GET SOME SLEEP!

Some of the wittiest dialogue heard
over the airwaves
during radio's golden age!

Written by
Philip Rapp

Foreword by Marsha Hunt

Edited by Ben Ohmart

BearManor Media
2004

The Bickersons Scripts: Volume 2
© 2004 by Paul Rapp
All rights reserved.

Foreword © 2004 by Marsha Hunt
Editor's Note © 2004 by Ben Ohmart

Published in the USA by

BearManor Media
P. O. Box 750
Boalsburg, PA 16827

bearmanormedia.com

Cover design by Joel Bogart
Cartoon reconstructions by Lloyd W. Meek
Typesetting and layout by John Teehan

Library of Congress Cataloging-in-Publication Data

Rapp, Philip.
The Bickersons scripts / written by Philip Rapp;
foreword by Marsha Hunt; edited by Ben Ohmart.
p. cm.
ISBN 1-59393-007-0 (pbk. : v. 2)

1. Bickersons (Radio program) 2. Radio plays, American. I. Ohmart, Ben. II. Title.

PS3568.A62925B53 2004
791.44'72--dc22
2004015092

ISBN—1-59393-007-0

Library of Congress Control No. 2004094188

Table of Contents

Recalling the Bickersons i
   by Marsha Hunt
Editor's Note iii

The Bickersons (Audition Show) – 1948 1
The Old Gold Show – January 23, 1948 23
The Old Gold Show – March 19, 1948 43
The Charlie McCarthy Show 61
The Bickersons – June 5, 1951 (Show #1) 67
The Bickersons – Show #5 (1951) 91
The Bickersons – Show #6 (1951) 109
The Bickersons – Show #9 (1951) 129
The Bickersons – Show #11 (1951) 149
TV Bit (Fireman John) 169
Coffee Rich Commercials 179
GM Commercial 187
Pream Commercials 189
RTA Commercials 195
Xmas Show 197

Recalling "The Bickersons"

"The Bickersons" radio sketches were a brief departure for me. When I was offered it I was home for awhile between Broadway plays, and I thought "Why not?" This would be good for me to try, a broad style of comedy I'd never played and didn't know much about. I had always enjoyed "light" comedy, with wit and subtlety and the well-turned phrase. This Bickerson material was vocal slapstick. Could I handle it?

I knew the role of Blanche rightly belonged to Frances Langford, who had created it but was then abroad and unavailable. Well, since she, an established singer, could succeed as the pestering, maddening Blanche, then maybe I, a serious actress, could too. I decided to plunge into those unfamiliar waters.

It proved to be a very good time, and a privilege to be a part of NBC's *Charlie McCarthy Show*. Everyone loved that character, that impudent dummy Charlie, who was anything but dumb. And it was utter delight to watch Edgar Bergen in action with him at the microphone. I also had great admiration for Ray Noble's music, not only as an orchestra sound, but for the marvelous songs he had written. Music is a major part of my life and I love and cherish that melodic kind of popular song that's been lost to us for the last few decades.

But getting back to the Bickersons, Don Ameche was a fine partner, a thorough professional who could — and did — play just about every kind of role. He came to the Bickersons character with the same wonderful verve and talent that he brought to all his varied portrayals. I guess we did click as a bickering couple, it turned out to be fun, and I wouldn't have missed it for anything.

– Marsha Hunt
April 2003

Editor's Note

Welcome to the second volume of Bickersons scripts! Though writer Phil Rapp reused much material during the 25-year career of The Bickersons, there is little here which replicates what you'll find in *The Bickersons Scripts Volume One*. Oh yes, you'll rediscover all of the best snoring, bourbon and bad cooking you can take here, but also a few surprises.

As before, I've tried to capture the true spirit of the original scripts, complete with formatting, to give a sense of historical accuracy. Rather than introduce each script, I wanted to take this opportunity to say a few words about this eclectic collection that basically runs the length of The Bickersons' life on radio and TV. Of course, for the full history of the team, you'll want to read my book: *The Bickersons – A Biography of Radio's Wittiest Program*.

The most difficult thing about splitting up what is essentially the entire Bickersons output into two separate volumes was the choice in routines. While some situations (and they were rare) were only written once (such as "Uncle Thurmond's Will" from *The Charlie McCarthy Show*), most of the text was recycled from *Drene Time* to *The Old Gold Show* to *The Bickersons* (1951) to various television skits. Sometimes there was no difference between scripts when going from series to series; sometimes there were subtle differences; sometimes (as in the case of the '51 series) there were significant additions that added a lot of new material to what was actually a tried-and-true situation. Deciding which version of sometimes six choices to include in this volume was a daunting task. But for the sake of variety, I tried to encompass a little of everything, from the '40s to the '70s.

Both volumes contain a lot of *The Bickersons* '51 because Philip Rapp was finally able to expand his pride and joy into a half-hour show, and therefore he wrote a lot more material for it, even though the series itself didn't last long. Many *Old Gold*s are also in these pages (and especially the first volume) because The Bickersons were new and Rapp was still experimenting with original plots and ways of keeping John awake all night. But the highlights for the die-hard Ameche-Langford fan must be the other goodies. Though Marsha Hunt replaced Frances Langford on a stretch of *Charlie McCarthy Show*s in 1948 that featured The Bickersons, much of that material was reworked from *Old Gold*s and therefore only one "original" bit was picked for this book. Also included is the Christmas show, in its 1970 incarnation when it seriously looked as though The Bickersons would have a shot at being a TV cartoon series. Another television routine is from an unknown show, but *had* to be included, as it's the only situation in which John Bickerson finds himself as a fireman!

The first time The Bickersons was up for its own half-hour series (1948), a special pilot was written, and is printed here for the first time. Perhaps the most surprising inclusions are the radio commercial scripts. Few people today realize that The Bickersons were kept busy well into the 1970s when Don Ameche and Frances Langford pitched everything from General Motors air conditioning to Coffee Rich. The 30- and 60-second spots were funny and popular, and proved to be an admirable swan song to a beloved creation.

Many theatre groups and radio recreation teams still request Bickersons scripts. Even though Don and Frances will remain the quintessential John and Blanche, obviously the strength of this hilarious marital hell is always firmly entrenched in the scripts. It was all about The Gags. It didn't and doesn't matter who snored or who screamed. These incredible, perfect dialogues are the stars.

— Ben Ohmart
March 2004

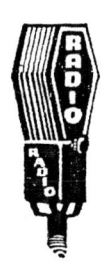

THE BICKERSONS (AUDITION SHOW) 1948

MAN: (YAWNING) Want the paper, Phyllis?

WOMAN: Thanks, honey...just put it down. I want to get some ginger ale. Want some?

MAN: No, thanks. Switch on the radio, will you, please?

WOMAN: It isn't nine yet, is it?

MAN: Just about. (YAWNS AGAIN) Why haven't we got a fireplace?

SOUND: RADIO IS SWITCHED ON

WOMAN: Gordon, honey, take your feet off the coffee table. Or take your shoes off, I'll bring your slippers.

MAN: Bring me some ginger ale, too. (PHONE RINGS...RECEIVER UP) Hello.

VOICE: (FILTER) Gordon?

MAN: What's doing, Ted?

(AT THIS POINT THE RADIO HAS WARMED UP AND FADES IN. DURING THE ENSUING TELEPHONE CONVERSATION THE RADIO PROGRAM WILL BE HEARD SIMULTANEOUSLY AND SLIGHTLY IN THE BACKGROUND)

VOICE: Nothing...What's new with you?

MAN: Nothing...Did you have dinner?

VOICE: Yeah. You gonna stay in?

ANNOUNCER: (Over music)...handled by our studio telephone operators. And to the lucky guesser of the mystery tune goes the grand jackpot prize consisting of a nine room home, complete with furniture and built-in Philco television, a thirty cubic foot Frigidaire freezer, a brand new Hudson convertible, a wild mink coat styled by I.J. Fox, a four-seater Navion flying station wagon—that's an airplane, folks—twelve-carat diamond ring straight from Cartier's, a trip for two to Naples on the White Star Line, a complete formal set of Community Silver, all sterling...

MAN:	Yeah, I think so, I wanna hear that whaddyacallit program. It's on now. I'll call you back in a little bit, Ted.
VOICE:	Okay…Hey, Gordon!
MAN:	Yeah?
VOICE:	Tell Phyllis Vivian got the felt for the hats, or something. I don't know.
MAN:	Okay.
SOUND:	HANGS UP
	(AT THIS POINT PHYLLIS HAS TWIRLED THE DIAL OF THE RADIO AWAY FROM THE GIVEAWAY PROGRAM AND IS SEARCHING FOR SOMETHING ELSE)
MAN:	Hey, Phyllis! What are you doing? Don't turn that off!
WOMAN:	It's nine o'clock…I want to get the Bickersons.
MAN:	What for? Don't you want to hear "Stop the Music"?
WOMAN:	You don't expect to win anything on that, do you?
MAN:	What do you expect to win on "The Bickersons"?
WOMAN:	Nothing. It just amuses me, that's all. I thought you liked the Bickersons.
MAN:	Yeah, but there's too much beefing all the time. Nobody talks like that. We've been married longer than they have and we never fight.
WOMAN:	That doesn't mean anything. We have a more placid nature.
MAN:	Put on "Stop the Music."
WOMAN:	You have a radio upstairs. Go up and listen to it. I want to hear the Bickersons.
MAN:	Phyllis, I just took my shoes off.
ANNCR:	(ON RADIO IN BACKGROUND)…starring Don Ameche and Frances Langford, as John and Blanche Bickerson, in "The Honeymoon Is Over."
MAN:	Oh, for heaven's sake!
SOUND:	SWITCHES DIAL
2ND ANNCR:	(ON RADIO) (STILL GOING STRONG)…a collapsible featherlight house trailer, a Kris Kraft Cabin Cruiser, complete with linens and crockery furnished by Cimble's Department Store and—
WOMAN:	You leave that dial alone, Gordon!

SOUND:	SWITCHES BACK TO BICKERSONS…BICKERSON THEME IS PLAYING
MAN:	(OVER BICKERSON THEME) Keep your hands off that radio, Phyllis!
WOMAN:	I'm going to listen to the Bickersons!
MAN:	Well, of all the stubborn, pigheaded, inconsiderate women—
WOMAN:	Don't you yell at me, you—you—why don't you yell at your boss? Maybe you'll get a little more money!
MAN:	In the whole twelve years we've been married I've been doing nothing but catering to you—I'm sick of it! Man can't even listen to a program—
WOMAN:	Oh, keep quiet.
MAN:	Ahh, nuts! Where's my shoes?
MUSIC:	(THEME OUT)
ANNCR:	As the minute hand of the clock gradually approaches seven A.M. John and Blanche Bickerson are in the breakfast room, which is also the living room and bedroom of their spacious one-room apartment. Mrs. Bickerson chatters, as husband John, ignoring his breakfast, attentively reads the morning paper.
LANG:	Well, why don't you answer me, John?
DON:	Mmm?
LANG:	If you'd take your head out of that paper for a minute you'd hear what I'm saying.
DON:	Always hear what you're saying.
LANG:	You do not. I might just as well be talking to a stone wall. You never listen to me. Your mind is always a million miles away.
DON:	Mmm.
LANG:	John.
DON:	Mmm.
LANG:	I've been signed up to go ten rounds with Joe Louis at Madison Square Garden.
DON:	Mmm.
LANG:	Yesterday the plumber discovered a radium mine under the bathroom sink.
DON:	Mmm.

LANG:	I put a nice big gob of poison in your orange juice this morning.
DON:	Mmm.
LANG:	Give me seven dollars to buy a new hat.
DON:	You don't need a new hat!
LANG:	It's a funny thing, but the minute I start talking about money, you can hear me fine.
DON:	I always hear you, Blanche. What did you say?
LANG:	I asked you why you came home so late last night?
DON:	I was working, Blanche. I told you I had to work overtime. Pour me some more coffee.
LANG:	That's tea. Did you get paid?
DON:	I'll get paid.
LANG:	What time did you get home?
DON:	Twelve-thirty.
LANG:	If you got home at twelve-thirty, why were you so long coming to bed? I know for a fact you didn't go to bed until almost two.
DON:	I was in the kitchen putting the stuff away.
LANG:	What stuff?
DON:	What's the matter, Blanche? You know you told me to bring stuff home for the party this afternoon. Your sister Clara's arriving from Chicago today and you told me to bring stuff! Well, I brought stuff!
LANG:	Did you bring potatoes for the potato salad?
DON:	I brought potatoes.
LANG:	Did you pare them?
DON:	I pared them.
LANG:	All of them?
DON:	All except one. It had a big knob on top and I couldn't find a mate for it.
LANG:	I meant did—
DON:	I know what you meant, Blanche. I peeled the potatoes and I even boiled them last night. They're in the icebox. Holy smoke, look at the time! Where's my hat?
LANG:	You're wearing it. What about your breakfast?

DON: What about it?

LANG: It's sitting there right in front of you and you never even looked at it.

DON: I looked at it.

LANG: Well, aren't you going to eat it?

DON: No, give it to your sister.

LANG: What's the matter with it?

DON: I never saw such stringy oatmeal in all my life.

LANG: That isn't oatmeal. It's chow-mein.

DON: Chow-mein! Who eats chow-mein for breakfast?

LANG: Well, I don't know what to give you. You won't eat normal breakfast food. You turn up your nose at stewed rabbit—you say you can't stand the sight of enchiladas—and you hate meatballs and spaghetti. What can I give you for breakfast?

DON: What's the matter with an egg, Blanche? An egg. That's all. Why can't I have an egg? There's plenty of ducks around!

LANG: You're the only man in town who eats duck eggs. I don't know where to buy them.

DON: Don't buy them. I don't like to eat breakfast. I never have an appetite in the morning, anyway. I gotta go, Blanche. It's late.

LANG: Here's a clean handkerchief. John, can't you take the afternoon off?

DON: What for?

LANG: Well, I think it's only proper for you to be here when Clara, Barney and the children arrive. We're the only relatives they've got, and you've never even seen them.

DON: I'll see them tonight.

LANG: Can't you come home little earlier? I'm sure they won't miss you if you take a few hours off. You're not *that* vital.

DON: I know it, but I don't want them to find it out. My job is hanging by a thread now.

LANG: I wish you'd find something more dignified, anyway.

DON: What do you mean—dignified? I'm getting paid, and that's all I care about.

LANG: Well, I don't like to go around telling people that I'm married to a billiard ball salesman.

DON:	Bowling balls!
LANG:	All right—bowling balls! I still think you can do better if you look around.
DON:	Goodbye, Blanche.
SOUND:	DOOR OPENS AND CLOSES
LANG:	John!
SOUND:	DOOR OPENS
DON:	What's the matter?
LANG:	That's a fine way to leave. Haven't you forgotten something?
DON:	Handkerchief…cigarettes…order blanks…samples…No—I've got everything.
LANG:	I mean is that the way a man says goodbye to his wife? Just goodbye?
DON:	Oh, honey, I can't shake hands with you now. I've got my fingers stuck in these bowling balls.
LANG:	Oh, goodbye!
SOUND:	DOOR SLAM
MUSIC:	(BRIDGE)
SOUND:	DISHES
LANG:	Did you like the chicken, Barney?
BARNEY:	Too much salt in it.
LANG:	Oh. Let me take those bones off your plate.
CLARA:	How about some more potato salad, Barney?
BARNEY:	Too many potatoes in it.
CLARA:	Isn't it awful to be married to a man like that, Blanche? He won't eat potato salad with potatoes in it. I have to fool him and make it with turnips.
LANG:	Oh, for heaven's sake, Clara. Well, it's certainly good to see you after all these years. Did you have a good trip?
CLARA:	Fine.
BARNEY:	(AT THE SAME TIME) Lousy.
CLARA:	Oh, how can you say that, Barney? It was a wonderful trip, and the children loved it.
BARNEY:	Four of us in an upper berth.

CLARA:	Oh, it wasn't bad at all, Blanche. Honest. None of us are big people, and little Ernie slept in the clothes hammock.
BARNEY:	Two-year-old kid—she lets him wander all over the train by himself.
CLARA:	Well, I couldn't take care of everything, Barney.
BARNEY:	When the train stopped at Albuquerque the kid locked himself in the washroom and wouldn't come out. The conductor was pounding on the window, but that was locked too.
LANG:	Well, what happened to him?
BARNEY:	We found him later walking around under the train. Still can't figure out how he got there.
LANG:	Did little George behave himself on the trip?
CLARA:	Like an angel. He can be an awful good boy when he wants to. He seemed rather pleased to get off at Pasadena and visit with Barney's sister, didn't he, Barney?
BARNEY:	No.
CLARA:	Well, your sister seemed pleased. They should be here pretty soon. How long does it take to get here from Pasadena, Blanche?
LANG:	By train?
CLARA:	Yes.
LANG:	Well, John works there and it never takes him over forty-five minutes. I thought George was going to stay in Pasadena for a while.
CLARA:	Well, I thought so, too. But after Eunice took a look at him she said she'd bring him back this evening.
BARNEY:	Which one of you two is older?
LANG:	What?
CLARA:	Oh, stop it, Barney! He wants to know everybody's age.
LANG:	Well, Clara's my older sister. Didn't you know that, Barney?
BARNEY:	No, I didn't know that. You look way older than Clara.
LANG:	(COLDLY) Really.
CLARA:	That's just his left-handed way of paying me compliments, Blanche. Barney, why don't you go back to the apartment and see if Ernie's still sleeping? I'll stay here and wait for George.
BARNEY:	Okay. I better take a little nap myself—I might have to look for a job next week. What's the number of that apartment house?
CLARA:	Two fourteen. The first apartment on the left. Go ahead.

BARNEY:	I'll take them chicken bones for Ernie—he's teething.
SOUND:	DOOR OPENS AND CLOSES
LANG:	You know, Clara, I had completely forgotten what Barney was like. He's awful little for a husband, isn't he?
CLARA:	Well, he may be small but he's wiry.
LANG:	Sort of outspoken, isn't he?
CLARA:	I'd rather have a man be frank about things than say one thing and mean another. Is John still as short-tempered as ever?
LANG:	Well—
CLARA:	Barney used to be that way before the children came. They changed everything. We haven't had a cross word since George was born.
LANG:	Is that so?
CLARA:	Blanche, I've often wondered. Why don't you and John—
LANG:	Oh, no, Clara—we can't afford it. I even thought of adopting a child, but there's so much red tape attached to it. They want to know how much you've got in the bank, what your husband does for a living, who your grandparents were. Honestly, trying to adopt a baby is almost as hard as getting an FHA loan.
CLARA:	Well, all I can tell you, Blanche, is that your married life would be much happier. You'd be surprised what a change would come over John if there was a child in the house.
LANG:	I know. A lot of people have told me that, Clara.
CLARA:	Blanche, I was just thinking—that apartment you got for us is rather small for four people.
LANG:	Well, it's the best I could do, Clara. And it's only temporary.
CLARA:	I know, dear—but I was just thinking…Why don't you let little George live with you for a while?
LANG:	George?
CLARA:	We'll be killing two birds with one stone. Our apartment will be less crowded and there'll be a big change in your married life.
LANG:	Maybe you're right, Clara. I'll call John at the office and tell him that we're going to have a baby.
MUSIC:	(BRIDGE)
SOUND:	TYPEWRITER…PHONE RINGS…TYPING STOPS…RECEIVER UP

MAN:	Acme Bowling Alley Equipment Company.
LANG:	(FILTER) Could I talk to Mr. Bickerson, please?
MAN:	Not in. He hasn't come off his route yet.
LANG:	Will you please leave word for him to call his wife as soon as he gets there?
MAN:	Okay.
LANG:	Thank you. Goodbye.
SOUND:	MAN HANGS UP…CONTINUES TYPING…DOOR OPENS AND CLOSES…FOOTSTEPS…TWO BOWLING BALLS DROP ON FLOOR AND ROLL…TYPING STOPS
MAN:	For the love of Pete! Look out where you drop those samples, Bickerson!
DON:	I couldn't carry them another minute! Why doesn't that cheap buzzard buy us cases for the darn things. My fingers look like a bunch of bananas.
MAN:	Call your wife. She just called here.
DON:	Yeah.
MAN:	Do any good today?
DON:	A waste of shoe-leather. I can't understand it…Here it is the height of the Christmas season and nobody is buying bowling balls.
MAN:	Nothing doing, huh?
DON:	No…Where is he?
MAN:	He went home early. It's been murder here today.
DON:	Aah, the old man don't bother me. He just lets off steam. His bark is worse than his bite.
MAN:	Well, he bit a few salesmen today.
DON:	So what? They come and they go. I've been here twelve years.
MAN:	Uh-huh.
DON:	Business has been bad before. Last year he lined up ten salesmen, took an 18-pound two-holer and chalked up a spare! I was the only salesman left standing.
MAN:	You were, huh?
DON:	Yeah, I was. He knows a good thing when he sees one.
MAN:	Uh-huh. Here's your pay envelope, Bickerson.

DON: Pay envelope? Today isn't payday.

MAN: It is for you.

DON: You're kidding.

MAN: No, I'm not. You got the axe.

DON: Holy smoke!

MAN: Don't take it so hard. I'll probably be next.

DON: I don't care for myself. It's what my wife's gonna say. She'll blow her cork.

MAN: What for? It's only a job.

DON: You don't understand. She's got her relatives here from Chicago—she's already figured on her Christmas shopping—and I haven't got fifty cents in the bank.

MAN: Well, I wish I could help you, Bickerson, but—

DON: I tell you I'm afraid to go home and face her. Do me a favor, will you, Marv?

MAN: Sure. What do you want me to do?

DON: Call up my wife and tell her.

MAN: You want me to tell her you were fired?

DON: Yes, but break the news very gently. First tell her I dropped dead then gradually work up to it.

MUSIC: (BRIDGE)

SOUND: STATION NOISES...CROWD...TRAIN BELL...ETC.

CONDUCTOR: (YELLS) Boooooooard!

SOUND: RUNNING FEET AS TRAIN STARTS TO MOVE OUT

DON: (BREATHLESS) Let me have a paper, willya, son...Quick...Here.

SOUND: CLAMBERS ON TRAIN...INSIDE EFFECT OF MOVING TRAIN

DON: Excuse me...Pardon me...I'm sorry...Is this seat taken, sonny?...Sonny—is this seat taken?

KID: No.

DON: Well, would you mind taking your feet off?

KID: Okay.

DON: Those packages, too.

KID:	Hah?
DON:	Would you please take those packages off the seat?
KID:	Just throw 'em on the floor.
DON:	Okay. (SWEEPS PACKAGES ONTO FLOOR) (MUTTERS) Wise little monkey! (OPENS HIS PAPER) Where's that Help Wanted page?
KID:	Hah?
DON:	Nothing! (READS TO HIMSELF) Accountant…Artist… Automobile salesman…Baker…Barber…Bartender…Book-keeper… Bartender!…BarTENDER!
KID:	What'll you have?
DON:	You mind your own business!
WOMAN:	Excuse *me*. You're sitting in my seat.
DON:	Huh? Oh, I'm sorry, Madam. Your son told me it wasn't taken.
WOMAN:	He's not my son.
KID:	And I didn't tell him it wasn't taken, either.
DON:	What!
KID:	I told him somebody was sitting here, and he knocked all your packages on the floor.
DON:	You told me this seat wasn't taken! And you told me to throw the packages on the floor!
KID:	I did not!
DON:	You did, too.
WOMAN:	You ought to be ashamed of yourself, trying to blame that little child.
MAN:	You can have my seat, Madam. I'm going into the smoking car.
WOMAN:	Thank you.
DON:	I'm sorry, really I am. Let me pick up those packages for you.
WOMAN:	Never mind. I'll get them myself. The very idea—Oh! Who did that?
KID:	He did it. I seen him pinch you.
DON:	Pinch who? What's the matter with you, you little muzzler.
WOMAN:	You just wait till the conductor comes by here.
2ND WOMAN:	Sit down here, dear. (CONFIDENTIALLY) I didn't like his looks from the minute he got on.

WOMAN:	I know the type. My husband's a correction officer.
DON:	(IN A LOW VOICE) What did you do that for?
KID:	Hah?
DON:	Why'd you tell that lady I pinched her? And why'd you tell me this seat wasn't taken? What did you tell me all those lies for?
KID:	Give me my bubble gum.
DON:	What bubble gum? I haven't got your bubble gum.
KID:	You have, too. It's stuck to your pants.
DON:	(SEETHING) Look at that! How'm I gonna get that off?
KID:	Give me my bubble gum.
DON:	Keep quiet till I get my knife out.
KID:	I want my bubble gum!
DON:	Stop pulling at my pants! (LOUD RIP) That's fine! That's just fine!
KID:	I want my bubble gum!
WOMAN:	Why don't you give the child his bubble gum?
DON:	He ripped my trousers!
KID:	Well, he pulled a knife on me!
DON:	Shut up, you little weasel!
KID:	(STARTS TO BAWL LUSTILY)
MAN:	What's going on here? You looking for trouble, Buddy?
DON:	Now wait a minute—
2ND WOMAN:	The man's a lunatic. He tried to stab the child!
DON:	You're out of your mind!
WOMAN:	Somebody pull the emergency cord!
	(AS THE MUSIC SNEAKS IN, THE KID CRIES...BABBLE OF EXCITED VOICES...DON PROTESTS...TRAIN STARTS TO SLOW DOWN)
MUSIC:	(SWELLS TO BRIDGE)
SOUND:	SLOW, MEASURED FOOTSTEPS GOING UPSTAIRS... THEY STOP
DON:	Oh, dear. (FOOTSTEPS CONTINUE) I should have stabbed the little brat, at that. Kids! No wonder tigers eat their young.

SOUND:	FOOTSTEPS STOP...KEY IN LOCK...DOOR OPENS AND CLOSES
LANG:	John! What happened to you? Your pants are torn—you're covered with dust—where have you been? I've been calling the office for hours.
DON:	(A DEAD VOICE) I got put off the train and I walked all the way home from Glendale.
LANG:	Well, what happened?
DON:	I don't want to talk about it. I don't even want to think about it. All I want to do is go to bed.
LANG:	Oh, you poor dear...And I have such a wonderful surprise for you.
DON:	Surprise?
LANG:	Yes, we're going to be the happiest couple in the world—and all because of my sister Clara.
DON:	What are you talking about?
LANG:	(AS SHE OPENS DOOR) George...come out and meet your new Daddy...Well, what do you think of him, John?
DON:	(BREATHES) Oh, no.
LANG:	Go on, sonny—kiss him.
KID:	Not me. That's the crook who stole my bubble gum!
MUSIC:	(BRIDGE...INTO NUMBER)
	APPLAUSE
MAN:	(OVER MUSIC) Hey, Phyllis—what time is it? Are you still listening to the Bickersons?
WOMAN:	Yes. How much did you win on "Stop the Music"?
MAN:	Ah, I fell asleep. (PHONE RINGS...RECEIVER UP) Hello?
VOICE:	(FILTER) Is their Mr. Gordon Leroy of 136 Flores?
MAN:	Yeah.
VOICE:	Have you been listening to "Stop The Music?
MAN:	(EXCITED) Yes...Yes...?
VOICE:	Can you identify our Mystery Tune?
MAN:	Wait a minute...Switch over to "Stop The Music" quick, Phyllis...Hello?
	(BAND CUTS OUT SUDDENLY)

ANNCR:	(ON RADIO)...A Maytag washing machine and ironer, five hundred pounds of eastern beef, a two and a half acre plot of radishes, twenty-one thousand dollars in government bonds...
SOUND:	RADIO CLICKS OFF
WOMAN:	Somebody's kidding you, Gordon.
MAN:	Hello?
VOICE:	(LAUGHS RAUCOUSLY) This is Ted, you jerk.
MAN:	Oh, are you funny! Why don't you grow up? (HANGS UP) Get the Bickersons back on again, will you, honey?
SOUND:	RADIO CLICKS BACK ON
MUSIC:	(THEME...SOFT AND PLAINTIVE)
ANNCR:	The Bickersons have retired. Blanche Bickerson tosses restlessly in the dark as poor husband John, unstrung by the events of the day, and suffering an attack of raucous insomnia, or Blaster's Phenomenon, engages in another losing battle with the dreaded ailment. Listen.
DON:	(SNORES LUSTILY...WHINES...SNORES AND WHINES)
LANG:	Oh, dear.
DON:	(SNORES AND GIGGLES)
LANG:	Oh, this is awful.
DON:	(SNORES AND GIGGLES MERRILY)
LANG:	I can't stand it. John! John!
DON:	(A PROTESTING WHINE) Mmmmmmmm.
LANG:	Stop it, stop it, stop it.
DON:	Stop it, Blanche. Wassamatter? Wassamatter, Blanche?
LANG:	There isn't another woman in the world who'd sacrifice her youth and her looks to live with a man who rattles himself to sleep like a lot of old bones in a bag. What do you think I am, John?
DON:	Old bag.
LANG:	What!
DON:	What? What'd you say, Blanche?
LANG:	I've never been so upset in all my life. Why couldn't the child live with us for a few weeks?
DON:	What child?
LANG:	George.

DON: Don't mention his name.

LANG: Well, you had no right to send him back to Clara. Clara and Barney are just sick about it.

DON: I can well imagine. Lemme sleep, Blanche.

LANG: I had him here for two hours before you got home and he was a perfect angel.

DON: Mmm.

LANG: What if he did make a little trouble on the train? He's a boy and all boys are kind of wild. Anyway, how did he know you were his uncle?

DON: What kind of an excuse is that?

LANG: I'm sure if you'd just try to understand him there wouldn't by any problem at all.

DON: That's what you think.

LANG: I don't think—I know.

DON: I don't think you know, either. The kid's gone—now forget about him.

LANG: I won't forget about him. And you needn't have made such an exhibition when you hauled him down the street to his mother.

DON: Ahhh!

LANG: That's no way to carry a boy, John.

DON: Well, I used to be a bowling ball salesman. Almost got my finger bit off.

LANG: What do you mean—used to be?

DON: Didn't he tell you? Didn't Marvin call you from the office?

LANG: Nobody called me from the office. What happened?

DON: I got fired.

LANG: Oh, John! What did you do that for?

DON: I didn't do it. The boss did it.

LANG: Well, he must have had a pretty good reason. I've felt this coming for a long time, John. You haven't had your mind on your work.

DON: Business was bad.

LANG: How can you say that? Prices are going up every day.

DON: Well, nobody's buying.

LANG: That's not true! I'm buying twice as much as I ever did! Business isn't bad with me.

DON: Goodnight, Blanche.

LANG: No! If you didn't do any business it's because you weren't concentrating on your work. You've just lost your ambition. You're not the same man I married, John. Whatever happened to your get-up-and-go?

DON: It got up and went.

LANG: I'll tell you what happened. You've lost interest in everything except that precious bourbon of yours!

DON: Now just a minute, Blanche—

LANG: I married a great big corkscrew!

DON: I resent that!

LANG: I don't care.

DON: You can accuse me of not being a good salesman, or not having ambition, or anything else—but drinking is not one of my failures!

LANG: No—it's one of your few successes!

DON: The only reason I use bourbon is because the doctor prescribed it! He said I would stop snoring if I took a jigger of bourbon and two aspirins every night.

LANG: That's not what you do, though.

DON: Yes it is!

LANG: It is not. You're six months behind on the aspirin and two years ahead on the bourbon.

DON: Well, aspirin gives me a headache. And bourbon has nothing to do with me losing my job.

LANG: Then why did you get fired?

DON: Because no man can serve two masters!

LANG: That's right—blame me! Since when do I boss you around? You know very well I let you have your own way in almost everything I want!

DON: You've been running me for years.

LANG: I have not!

DON: It started right at the altar! When I said "I do" you said "Oh, no you don't!"

LANG: How can you lie there and deliberately make up such—

DON: Well, don't rile me up. If you'd just sympathize with me when I get a bad break instead of hounding me our marriage would work a lot better. Matrimony is a serious thing!

LANG:	You're a fine one to talk about matrimony! You don't know the meaning of the world.
DON:	It's not a word—it's a sentence.
LANG:	Oh, you poor thing. How you suffer! I didn't get such a bargain, you know. There's better fish in the ocean than the one I caught!
DON:	There's better bait, too.
LANG:	Then it's true! You don't love me and you never did!
DON:	Oh, I did, too!
LANG:	What?
DON:	I mean I do, too!
LANG:	You don't, you don't, you don't!
DON:	Blanche, I do!
LANG:	Well, you never say it!
DON:	I say it a thousand times a day!
LANG:	Well, say it now!
DON:	I love you.
LANG:	Will you love me as long as you live?
DON:	Yes.
LANG:	Swear. Swear you'll love me as long as you live.
DON:	Cross my heart and hope to die!
LANG:	That has a double meaning.
DON:	Well, I only meant it one way.
LANG:	It's really an effort for you to show any kind of affection for me, isn't it, John? Why are you so ashamed to tell me you love me?
DON:	I'm not ashamed, Blanche. I just can't seem to convince you, that's all. You know I love you so.
LANG:	So what?
DON:	That's what I say—who cares! Put out the lights and go to sleep.
LANG:	If only you'd let me know that you appreciate what I do for you.
DON:	Oh, you don't do so much for me.
LANG:	Is that so? Who cooks for you? I do! Who cleans for you? I do! Who does your laundry?

DON: The laundry.

LANG: Only once and that was because the washing machine was broken. If it wasn't for me you wouldn't have a clean shirt.

DON: I haven't got a clean shirt.

LANG: You have too. I dusted one off yesterday.

DON: Dusted it off is right. And you pressed the collar with a curling iron. Besides, I wore it today.

LANG: Today? What happened to the shirt you wore Tuesday?

DON: I wore it Wednesday. And I was going to wear it again Saturday, but I spilled some gravy on it Friday, so I cut the stain out and made a brown collar for my Sunday shirt.

LANG: Oh, stop complaining. You've got two lovely shirts.

DON: One shirt. And it's not lovely. It hasn't even got a shirt-tail.

LANG: You don't need a shirt-tail. Just wear your pants higher.

DON: I can't wear 'em any higher. I wear my pants so high now I have to unzip 'em to blow my nose.

LANG: I can just hear you raising your voice to Gloria Gooseby!

DON: Now don't start with Gloria Gooseby!

LANG: Believe me, if you were around her for a little while you'd cool off in a hurry.

DON: I've been around her for hours and I never cool off! I mean, I despise Gloria Gooseby and I wouldn't have anything to do with her.

LANG: Then why does she keep staring at you like she's hypnotized?

DON: She doesn't stare. It's just that she wears those outlandish dresses and they bring out her eyes!

LANG: They bring out yours, too! No wonder all you men gawk at her. All her gowns are strapless and backless. Would you like me to dress like that?

DON: Mmm.

LANG: Maybe I should. I wonder how I'd look in a gown that's strapless and backless?

DON: Skinless and boneless.

LANG: I'll never forgive you for that remark, John Bickerson.

DON: I'm sorry. I'm so tired I don't know what I'm saying. Why don't you let me sleep, Blanche?...Where you going?

LANG:	I'm leaving this house and I'm never coming back.
DON:	Blanche—wait a minute! Come back here! What's the matter with you?
LANG:	It's no use, John. We'll keep on fighting like this. I tried to make our lives more pleasant by bringing little George here, but you wouldn't have him.
DON:	All right. I'll go get him in the morning.
LANG:	You say it, but you won't do it. Do it now!
DON:	What?
LANG:	Go on. Get up and bring George back.
DON:	Blanche, are you out of your mind? It's four o'clock in the morning!
LANG:	Either you bring George back or I'm leaving.
DON:	Nobody would believe this!...Where's my clothes?
LANG:	Just throw my kimono over your pajamas. They only live down the street—Two fourteen. The first apartment on the left.
DON:	I know I'll wake up and find this is all a bad dream.
LANG:	Go on...take a flashlight so you don't have to put any lights on. I'll phone Clara and tell her you're coming.
SOUND:	DOOR OPENS...SOUND OF DIALING...DOOR CLOSES
MUSIC:	(BRIDGE)
SOUND:	HESITANT FOOTSTEPS ON STREET
DON:	Two fourteen...Where's two fourteen?...Wish they'd put some street lights in this crummy neighborhood. Broken-down flashlight's no good—the batteries are dead. Can't see your hand in front of your face.
COP:	Looking for something?
DON:	Huh?...Oh, hello, officer. Shine that light around a little bit—I'm looking for number 214.
COP:	Live there?
DON:	No...No. Just looking. Why?
COP:	Not everybody walks around at three o'clock in the morning wearing a pink kimono and carrying a bottle of bourbon.
DON:	Bottle of bourbon? No wonder it wouldn't light. Dear heaven, I almost threw it away!

COP:	What's that?
DON:	I picked it up by mistake…I thought it was a flashlight. Well, it's not a total loss…Will you join me, officer?
COP:	No thanks, I'm off duty. Two fourteen's right on the corner. You'd better keep moving so you don't catch cold.
DON:	Yeah…I better wrap this bourbon around me a little tighter.
MUSIC:	(BRIDGE)
DON:	The first apartment on the left…(OPENS DOOR) I hope I don't wake anybody up…Wish I could put on the light…Where is the little dear?…Here he is—sleeping like an innocent newborn vulture…Well, here goes. (GRUNTS AS HE LIFTS HIS BURDEN)
MUSIC:	(BRIDGE)
SOUND:	FOOTSTEPS OF A MAN CARRYING A HEAVY LOAD
DON:	This kid's heavier than I thought…Only another ten yards.
COP:	Pick up a friend?
DON:	Oh. Is that you, officer?
COP:	Yes, it's me. May I ask what you have in the bundle?
DON:	It's my nephew. I'm bringing him home to my wife. It's a long story, officer—but I assure you, this is nothing anybody would want to steal.
COP:	Uh-huh. Well, you better watch how you got those blankets wrapped around his head. He's liable to smother.
DON:	(AFTER A SIGNIFICANT PAUSE…HOPEFULLY) You think so?…Thanks, officer. Goodnight.
MUSIC:	(BRIDGE)
SOUND:	KICKING AT DOOR
DON:	(HOARSE WHISPER) Blanche! Open up! (DOOR OPENS) He weighs a ton. Put on the lights.
LANG:	No. It'll wake him. Keep your voice down.
DON:	What'll I do with him?
LANG:	I've got the cot all ready in the kitchen. Put him down gently, John.
DON:	(PUTS HIM DOWN) There. There's your new son—you've just become a mother. Are you satisfied?
LANG:	Sshhh. Go on into your own bed…Now I can sleep.

DON: (SETTLING INTO BED) What a day...I lost my job...I got thrown off a train...I deliver children at four o'clock in the morning...Oh, dear.

(THERE IS A LOUD SUSTAINED SNORE)

LANG: Oh, John! Must you start snoring as soon as you close your eyes?

DON: (OVER ANOTHER SNORE) Snoring? Who's snoring? I'm not snoring! It's that darn kid, that's who it is.

(SNORING CONTINUES THROUGH SCENE)

LANG: George?

DON: Yes, George! Go turn him over on his side!

LANG: (JUMPS OUT OF BED) Well, I never! Turn over, George dear...John!

DON: What's the matter?

LANG: This isn't George—you brought back Barney!

DON: Why was I ever born!

MUSIC: (THEME)

(APPLAUSE)

THE OLD GOLD SHOW

a Lennen & Mitchell Radio Production

Sponsor P. LORRILLAND CO.
308 N. Rodeo Drive, Beverly Hills, Calif.

Station CBS   **Date** 1/23/48   **Time** 6:00-6:30 PM   **Studio** VINE ST.

Cast	Music Routine
FRANK MORGAN	OPENING THEME
DON AMECHE	
FRANCES LANGFORD	MORGAN PLAYOFF
CARMEN DRAGON	
FRANK GOSS	BICKERSON THEME
MARVIN MILLER	BICKERSON PLAYOFF
EVELYN SCOTT	CLOSING THEME
SIX HITS AND A MISS	
A. K. SHOWALTER	

REVISED

(ON CUE)

MILLER: From Hollywood—it's Old Gold Cigarette Time.

CHORUS: Treat yourself…to Old Golds.

GROUP: If you want a treat instead of a treatment.

CHORUS: Treat yourself…to Old Golds.

GROUP: If you want a treat instead of a treatment.

CHORUS: Treat yourself…
Treat yourself…
Treat yourself…to Old Golds.

MILLER: If you want a treat instead of a treatment…

TREAT YOURSELF TO A PACK OF OLD GOLDS!

(PAUSE)

MUSIC: (THEME…ESTABLISH AND FADE UNDER FOLLOWING)

MILLER: This is Marvin Miller, ladies and gentlemen, speaking for the makers of Old Gold cigarettes who are pleased to present the eighteenth in a series of new programs with Carmen Dragon and his orchestra, starring Metro-Goldwyn-Mayer's loveable Frank Morgan, the genial Don Ameche and charming Frances Langford, who sings—

MUSIC: LANGFORD AND ORCH…"THERE'LL BE SOME CHANGES MADE"

(APPLAUSE)

FIRST COMMERCIAL

MILLER: The best way to smoke is to smoke for pleasure. And the best way to get your smoking pleasure is through an Old Gold. Today… why not start enjoying the wonderful pleasure of an Old Gold…its taste…its smoothness…and mildness. After all…Old Golds are an exclusive blend of the world's choice tobaccos…product of nearly two hundred years' experience with fine quality tobaccos. So…today…find out about Old Golds! Because listen…if you want to smoke for the wonderful pleasure of it…if you want a treat instead of a treatment…

CHORUS: Treat yourself…to Old Golds

GROUP: …if you want a treat instead of a treatment

CHORUS: Treat yourself…to Old Golds!

MILLER Now here is your host for the evening, Don Ameche.

(APPLAUSE)

AMECHE: Thank you, ladies and gentlemen, and good evening. These days a matter of great concern to most Californians is the weather. As you all know, we've been without rain for quite some time, and—

DRAG: That's news to me, boy.

LANG: Oh, Carmen, you must know it hasn't rained for two months.

DRAG: How would I know? I never read the weather reports.

AMECHE: What?

DRAG: You heard me. By the time I get through with Li'l Abner and Dick Tracy my wife's got the garbage wrapped up in the rest of the paper—and I can't unwrap it just to find out if it's raining. Furthermore—

LANG: Please, Carmen—Don wants to introduce the guest.

DRAG: Why did he hire a garbage collector, anyway?

AMECHE: He's no garbage collector! He's a meteorologist.

DRAG: Oh.

AMECHE: Ladies and gentlemen, the weatherman is a person who, for many years has been the butt of jokes and ridicule—while his scientific training is completely overlooked. However, now that Southern California is undergoing the driest period since 1877, while blizzards have blanketed the East with snow, all eyes are glued to the man who predicts the weather. So tonight it's my pleasure to present the Chief Weather Forecaster for Los Angeles—Mr. A. K. Showalter. Mr. Showalter.

(APPLAUSE)

SHOW: Thank you.

AMECHE: Mr. Showalter, before we go any further, I'd like to have you meet some of the people on our show. This is Frances Langford.

SHOW: This is a real pleasure, Miss Langford. I'd like to say that you're even prettier than you sound over the air

LANG: Thank you.

DRAG: Some weatherman. She's fair and he's warmer.

AMECHE: All right, Carmen. Mr. Showalter, this is our orchestra leader, Carmen Dragon.

SHOW: How do you do, Mr. Dragon?

DRAG: Harya. Did you hear about the Mexican Weather Report?

SHOW: Mexican Weather Report?

DRAG: Yare. Chile today and hot tamale. Anything?

AMECHE: Go away, Carmen. Mr. Showalter, how do you weather men arrive at a forecast?

SHOW: Well, we use a weather map which is plotted from the data we receive from our observers. Here's an old one you can look at.

AMECHE: Oh, yes. What are all these crayon marks?

SHOW: They indicate the warm fronts and cold fronts. There's the high pressure area—and there's the low. These black concentric ovals are called isobars.

AMECHE: Very complex. Is this your forecast written at the bottom?

SHOW: That's it.

LANG: What does it say, Don?

AMECHE: Big wind approaching.

MORG: (COMING ON) I heard that, Dodger—and it's a dastardly way to announce my entrance!

AMECHE: Frank!

(APPLAUSE)

MORG: I won't have you kicking me in the face when my back is turned! Why must I—

AMECHE: Frank! Stop beating your gums. We were just discussing the bum weather with this gentleman.

MORG: Oh, he's a weather-beaten bum. Well, he sure looks it! Who let him in?

SHOW: Please, Mr. Morgan, I—

MORG: I'm sorry, my good man — I never give handouts to tramps. However, if you're willing to sweep out my dog kennel I might—

LANG: Oh, Mr. Morgan! There's no tramp here.

MORG: That's an understatement if I ever heard...Oh, hello, my dear!

LANG: Hello.

MORG: Well, this is a rare treat! I haven't seen you since I squeezed you at the Pasadena Orange Festival.

LANG: Orange Festival?

MORG: Yes. Aren't you Miss Pulp of 1947? I hardly recognised you without your smudgepots...Why don't you visit my orchard tomorrow?

LANG: Well, I—

MORG: Come early. You'll find my citrus grove in Boyle Heights right opposite the Corned Beef Factory.

LANG: Corned Beef Factory?

MORG: Yes. Bring your own brisket—basket. We'll pick a few Valencias and I'll let you examine my Sunkist Navels.

LANG: Well, I can't make it, but my husband Jon Hall is insane about citrus.

MORG: Oh—husband's insane.

LANG: One hour with him and he'll spray your trunks, trim up your limbs and pull down your plants! Goodnight, gentlemen. (SHE GOES)

MORG: What happened?

AMECHE: Frank, you've done it again! That was Frances Langford, Old Gold's star singer, and it's high time you recognised her.

MORG: Err—Goldie Highfinger. Old wreck. Well—Oh, dear!

AMECHE: What's wrong, Morgan?

MORG: Dodger, I owe that young lady an apology. I want it understood that I was just engaging in a bit of harmless banter with her. Actually, I'm afraid of women.

AMECHE: You're afraid of women?

MORG: Yes—I just saw my wife sitting in the audience. Well, I think I'll be running—

SHOW: Just a minute, Mr. Morgan—

MORG: I told you son—I've got no time for panhandlers. Not one with a pan like yours, anyway. I've got to—

AMECHE: Frank, are you going to run away without even talking to this gentleman?

MORG: Well, I can't be giving quarters to every seedy bum I meet. Why doesn't he get a job?

AMECHE: He's got a job! An important one, too. He'll be the most popular man in California when the showers arrive.

MORG: Is that your business, son?

SHOW: Yes, sir.

MORG: Well, I wish you'd visit my bathroom sometime. I've got a leaky faucet and the tub keeps overflowing. We've got beer bottles floating all over the house.

SHOW: Mr. Morgan, the bathtub should not be used for chilling beer. During the present drought all conscientious Californians should be wise enough to conserve water.

MORG: What?

SHOW: That's merely the opinion of a civil servant.

MORG: Well, I'll thank you to be more civil, servant. I was only trying to find out what you do for a living.

SHOW: I'm sorry, Mr. Morgan. I spend most of my time on the roof with a rain gage and a tipping bucket.

MORG: Well, you needn't be ashamed of your calling, my boy. I had an uncle who was a wet nurse in a fish hatchery. He handled nothing but halibut and smelt.

AMECHE: Smelt?

MORG: Something awful. Poor old codger got his head caught in a drainpipe and was swept into the reservoir with two thousand other crappies. Our whole family gave up drinking water after that.

	What are you doing here?
SHOW:	Mr. Ameche invited me. Just before you came in he was inspecting my map. Would you like to examine it?
MORG:	I have—and I find it ghastly. Why don't you wear a diving helmet?
AMECHE:	He's talking about a weather map, sap!
MORG:	Oh, mapsap. Weather!
AMECHE:	From the Los Angeles Weather Bureau. You can look at it if you think it'll make any sense to you. Here.
MORG:	Hmmmm. Very interesting. (TO HIMSELF) Low pressure area latitude 45 North, longitude 135 East...Polar easterly on semipermanent Pacific High...Hmmmm...(BEGINS TO ENJOY IT) Whirling storm temperate zone...(MUMBLES AND LAUGHS) ...rising barometric pressure. Who made this childish map?
AMECHE:	The Chief Weather Forecaster for Los Angeles—Mr. Showalter.
MORG:	Don't tell me they took that phoney back!
SHOW:	Phoney? Do you know Albert Kenneth Showalter?
MORG:	Just well enough to call him A. K.! I fired him in 1929 when I took the Bureau over.
AMECHE:	What? What's this about you taking over the Bureau, Morgan?
MORG:	You needn't act so startled, Dodger. Washington got fed up with the unreliable weather reports from here—and my record as an expert meteorologist left the government only one course—of course.
AMECHE:	Of course—
MORG:	Of course. It's true another climatic expert was being considered for the important post, a man highly proficient in snow conditions—
AMECHE:	In Los Angeles.
MORG:	Precisely. But my uncanny forecasts of impending hail swayed the board so they turned down the man with the snow.
SHOW:	And they took you?
MORG:	Yes—their decision was the hail with Morgan. (EXAMINING SCRIPT) What?
AMECHE:	What about this Showalter, Frank?
MORG:	I gave him a job as my assistant to keep him from starving to death.
SHOW:	This comes as quite a shock to me, Mr. Morgan.

MORG:	It wouldn't be a shock to you, sir, if you knew this Shawlwhacker.
SHOW:	Showalter.
MORG:	Yes. A more thoroughly inefficient lout never bribed his way through a Civil Service examination! Light-fingered, too.
SHOW:	What!
MORG:	Yes—a little matter of stealing postage stamps.
AMECHE:	Did you catch him stealing the stamps, Frank?
MORG:	No, but he certainly mailed a lot of letters for a fellow who had no friends. I might have overlooked even that if he had the slightest idea of how to make a forecast. I'll never forget his first miserable attempt at a weather report.
AMECHE:	What did it say?
MORG:	"Possibly cooler Saturday, most likely followed by Sunday." I don't have to tell you it was the only time in history that Monday followed Saturday!
SHOW:	You mean this—this—
MORG:	Faker.
SHOW:	Yes. This faker, Showalter, doesn't know anything about meteorology?
MORG:	Well, I'd be willing to wager he knows even less about it than you do—if such a thing is possible. And when I look at you, anything's possible!
AMECHE:	Wonderful world!
MORG:	The man had just completed a graduate course at M.I.T. and still I had to instruct him how to take hourly readings on the anemometer and hygrometer.
AMECHE:	What's an anemometer and a hygrometer?
MORG:	Well, err—
SHOW:	An anemometer is used to determine wind velocity, and a hygrometer measures moisture in the air.
MORG:	Yes. I told—you know something about weather forecasting, son?
SHOW:	About as much as Showalter.
MORG:	Oh. You had me nervous for a minute. Well, it didn't take me long to find out this chap was unable to check his wind and water. The man knew absolutely nothing about thodolites and radiosondes, but oddly enough, when he predicted rain—it rained. I found out

	later he was depending on a corn in his left big toe! Well, I can't talk about that idiot anymore, so I'll—
AMECHE:	Don't run, Frank. Wouldn't you like to know who this gentleman is?
MORG:	Dodger, I've told you time and again, your ignorant friends don't inter—oh! I—feel a storm brewing! Don't tell me this is—
AMECHE:	Yes. You'll be glad to know this is A.K. Showalter—Chief Weather Forecaster of the Los Angeles Meteorological Bureau.
MORG:	Oh—meteor—glad. Glad to meteor. See you again. I've got to—
AMECHE:	Come back here, you faker! Apologize to Mr. Showalter for all those lies.
SHOW:	That isn't necessary, Don. I'm sure Mr. Morgan was just pulling my leg.
MORG:	Why, bless your leg, of course! I recognized you instantly, Mr. Saltwater—
SHOW:	Showalter.
MORG:	Yes. It's just that I haven't seen you since the Weatherman's Convention in Cloudburst, Indiana. Did you ever get your pants back?
AMECHE:	You see, Mr. Showalter—you give this windbag half a chance—
MILLER:	I don't like to intrude, Don. But it seems to me you might treat Mr. Morgan with a little more respect.
MORG:	Well! What a perfect interruption. You're that plump young poultry chef from the Tail O' The Cock. Pull up a goose and stuff it.
MILLER:	Pardon?
MORG:	Come, come, don't hold out on me, my boy. I'm sure you've got some fricassee in that enormous pot under your vest.
AMECHE:	Why don't you stop it, Frank! You know very well he's our announcer.
MORG:	He is? He doesn't look like that overweight slopbucket, Marvin Miller.
MILLER:	That's me. I'm that overweight slopbucket, Mr. Morgan.
MORG:	My apologies, sir. Allow me to introduce you to the Chief Weather Forecaster for Los Angeles. Mr. Waterbowl, this is Mr. Slopbucket.
MILLER:	Mr. Waterbowl.
SHOW:	Mr. Slopbucket.
AMECHE:	Frank! Where did you get the Waterbowl and Slopbucket?

MORG:	I don't know—there must be something wrong with the plumbing.
MILLER:	Mr. Morgan, I don't want to bother you—
MORG:	Well, you do, you know.
MILLER:	I'm sorry, but I heard you discussing weather reports and I've been a student of meteorology for years. Just lately I've been having trouble with my barometric charts.
MORG:	(BORED) Mmm.
MILLER:	I manage to control my low pressure area, and I can cope with my fluctuating moisture, but I don't know how to prognosticate a cold front.
MORG:	Why don't you try using a hot water bottle?
AMECHE:	Oh, I've had enough of this! Mr. Showalter, I hope you'll forgive me for subjecting you to all of Morgan's nonsense about being a weather forecaster.
MORG:	Now see here, Dodger—
AMECHE:	Go on! You couldn't predict a burp after a Hungarian dinner.
MORG:	Nonsense! The Morgans have been weather experts for years beginning with Grandfather Drizzle Morgan, down to my Uncle Snowball and my Aunt Slush.
AMECHE:	Your Aunt Slush?
MORG:	A slippery old pile. Always oozed off the trunks when she was loaded.
MILLER:	What a wonderful family.
MORG:	Yes. I was still in knee-pants when I was summoned before the Royal Barometric Society in London to demonstrate the Morgan Method for dissolving fog.
SHOW:	What did you do?
MORG:	While a large and admiring crowd gathered to watch my new technique, I uncorked a bottle of specially prepared alcohol and in ten minutes I weakened and dissipated a stubborn miss. Mist!
MILLER:	I knew you meant mist, Mr. Morgan.
MORG:	Did you really!
MILLER:	Yes. Please tell us some more about your experiments with the weather, Mr. Morgan.
MORG:	Oh, well—all right. While I was still a young man I discovered that I was one of the few strangely endowed humans known as rainmakers.

SHOW: Oh, yes.

MORG: Oh, yes, he says. My services were in demand to produce rain from Maine to California, and it has been recorded that I have never been found in a dry state. (I think there's a double meaning there!)

AMECHE: If there is, I only got one of them. How did you go about making rain, Barrel?

MORG: Oh, rainbarrel. Well, I inherited a secret device from my grandfather who had employed a principle used centuries before by the Zulu pigmies. His tools were crude and undeveloped, but he had a brain to match them.

AMECHE: I guess you inherited that, too.

MORG: I guess so—no! Dodger, I won't stand here and—

MILLER: Please go on, Mr. Morgan. If Don interrupts you again I'll lean on him.

MORG: Very well. I began my experiments in secret and after my first nine hundred failures I suspected I was on the wrong track. I was about to convert my rainmaking machine into a grain still—mill—when word reached me that Kansas was suffering the worst drought in history. Immediately, I began the trek on foot, lugging along my huge rainmaking machine.

SHOW: Where did you live at the time?

MORG: In Kansas. The drought was killing livestock and crops and ruining farms and homesteads—

AMECHE: Must have been pretty dry.

MORG: Dry! After milking a cow for three hours all I got was a bucket of sand. But I was determined to make my experiment a successful one. I set my machine up in a deserted barn, locked myself from the prying eyes of the skeptical farmers, whom I had charged a dollar apiece, and promised them rain within twenty-four hours!

SHOW: What happened?

MORG: Stop breathing down my neck, son. As the hours ticked slowly by, the crowd outside the barn became larger and more restive. Still the sun beat down with fierce gloating. The truculent people began arming themselves with clubs and rocks, to present to me should I fail.

SHOW: Well?

MORG: Two minutes before the twenty-fourth hour the skies grew leaden—clouds began to form—

AMECHE:	Uh-huh.
MORG:	As the last second struck—a huge farmer electrified the crowd by declaring he'd caught a drip!
MILLER:	It was rain!
MORG:	No—it was me—I was trying to sneak out the back door!...Well, so long, fellows, I gotta buy an umbrella.
MUSIC:	MORGAN PLAYOFF
	(APPLAUSE)
MUSIC:	INTRO "SERENADE OF THE BELLS"
MILLER:	(OVER THEME) Frances Langford sings "Serenade of the Bells."
MUSIC:	ORCH AND LANGFORD..."SERENADE OF THE BELLS"
	(APPLAUSE)
CHORUS:	Treat yourself...to Old Golds.
GROUP:	...if you want a treat instead of a treatment.
CHORUS:	Treat yourself...to Old Golds.
GROUP:	...if you want a treat instead of a treatment.
CHORUS:	Treat yourself...to Old Golds.
MILLER:	There's only one way to find out if Old Golds are tastier, smoother, milder than any cigarette you know! And that is...to smoke a pack of Old Golds. And then you'll know...that you simply cannot match the quality of an Old Gold!
WOMAN:	Today's the day to find out about Old Golds!
MILLER:	Yes! Of course...today...discover the wonderful pleasures of smoking an Old Gold! Find out what it really means to smoke a cigarette that's tastier...smoother...milder! Actually...the quality of an Old Gold cannot be duplicated! Because no other cigarette in America has the quality traditions of an Old Gold. Listen...
2d ANN:	Nearly two hundred years of fine tobacco experience are behind every Old Gold you smoke. We're tobacco men...not medicine men. Old Golds cure just one thing...tobaccos...the world's choice tobaccos...to give you a milder smoke...a better-tasting smoke!
WOMAN:	Today's the day to find out about Old Golds!
MILLER:	Yes, yes, yes! You owe it to your sweet pleasure's sake to get more smoking pleasure. So smoke a pack of Old Golds...today! Because if you want a treat instead of a treatment...

CHORUS: Treat yourself...to Old Golds.

GROUP: ...if you want a treat instead of a treatment.

CHORUS: Treat yourself...to Old Golds.

MILLER: Now here are Don Ameche and Frances Langford as John and Blanche Bickerson in "The Honeymoon is Over."

THEME: (SOFT AND PLAINTIVE)

MILLER: For many years, John Bickerson, victim of a rare type of insomnia, has refused medical aid to alleviate his sleepless condition. Tonight, Mrs. Bickerson has taken matters in her own hands and three o'clock in the morning finds Dr. Hersey preparing to treat the unfortunate John as he reaches the crisis during an acute attack of his ailment. Listen.

DON: (SNORES LUSTILY...WHINES...SNORES AND WHINES...BROKEN RHYTHM SNORE FOLLOWED BY A WHINE)

LANG: Honest, doctor, it's like being married to a Diesel engine.

DOC: Would you roll up his pyjama sleeve, please?

DON: (SNORES AND GIGGLES...SNORES AND GIGGLES AGAIN)

DOC: Higher.

DON: (SNORES AND GIGGLES MERRILY)

LANG: Oh, I can't look, doctor.

DOC: He won't feel it...(SMALL GRUNT)

DON: (SMALL SQUEAL)

LANG: Is it over?

DOC: Not quite. I'm giving him fifty cc's....There. That'll do it.

DON: (SNORES)

LANG: He's still snoring.

DOC: (DROPS SYRINGE INTO A BASIN) It's rapid, but not that rapid, Mrs. Bickerson. (DON SNORES THRU THIS) But once the injection takes effect it'll bring relief for several hours.

ANG: I hope so. I sure need relief.

DOC: He's subsiding now.

DON: (A MODERATE SIZE SNORE THAT DIES AWAY COMPLETELY)

LANG:	He's stopped!
DOC:	Yes.
LANG:	What is that stuff, doctor? It's magic! I can't believe it.
DOC:	I'm a little startled myself. It's the first time I've ever tried it.
LANG:	It isn't dangerous, is it?
DOC:	Oh no. It's just a mild mydriatic alkaloid combined with oil of garlick. It produces a change in the blood pressure and has a secondary effect as a vasoconstrictor. I've given him enough to stop him at least for eight hours.
LANG:	Are you sure he's breathing?
DOC:	(LAUGHS REASSURINGLY) It's just that you've become accustomed to his stertor, Mrs. Bickerson. Of course he's breathing—very quietly and with great regularity. Listen closely.
DON:	(SNORES LIKE A STEAM SHOVEL...HUMS AND CLUCKS)
LANG:	The garlic's working, anyway.
DOC:	Hmm. Must have used a dull needle.
DON:	(SNORES...HUMS AND CLUCKS)
DOC:	Amazing. I'll have to try a stronger solution. Call me in the morning. Goodnight, Mrs. Bickerson.
LANG:	Goodnight, doctor. (DOOR CLOSES) There's only one way to stop him from snoring. John...John!
DON:	Mmm.
LANG:	Turn over on your side. Go on!
DON:	(A PROTESTING WHINE)
LANG:	Stop it, stop it, stop it!
DON:	Stop it, Blanche. Wassamatter? Whattaya pulling at me for?
LANG:	Turn over on your side.
DON:	Can't sleep on my side—hurts. Too lumpy.
LANG:	It wouldn't be so lumpy if you'd unstrap that bottle of bourbon from your pyjamas. Take it off!
DON:	(WHINING) Leave it alone, Blanche. Lemme sleep.
LANG:	I was humiliated beyond words. Dr. Hersey was just here and he saw that bottle.

DON: Mmm.

LANG: He gave you a shot.

DON: Nice man. Did he put the cork back?

LANG: He gave you a shot in the arm. An injection.

DON: Waste of good liquor.

LANG: John! Do you hear what I'm telling you? Dr. Hersey was here and he gave you an injection with a hypodermic needle.

DON: Whaffor?

LANG: To stop you from snoring. He gave you some oil of something mixed with a little garlic juice. How do you feel?

DON: Like a salad.

LANG: Don't be funny!

DON: Lemme sleep, willya, Blanche—I'm exhausted. Goodnight.

LANG: No! I can't stand another minute of it, John. You rattle away every night like a metal freight car loaded with bolts and nuts.

DON: Nuts.

LANG: This strain is just too much for me.

DON: Mmm.

LANG: I've tried to get away from your snoring by sleeping in the bathroom—in the kitchen—last week I slept in the hall. What other man makes his wife sleep in the hall, John?

DON: Jon Hall. Put the lights out, Blanche.

LANG: I will not! You tell everyone you've got insomnia but I'm the one who doesn't sleep. I never close my eyes.

DON: Can't sleep unless you close your eyes.

LANG: What good does it do to close them? You only shake me out of my skin with that hideous snoring of yours.

DON: Blanche, it's just your imagination. I never snore and you know it.

LANG: Never snore! The second day of our honeymoon I couldn't hear the Falls!

DON: You didn't miss anything.

LANG: Something has to be done, John. Dr. Hersey's just about given up hope.

DON: Blanche, did you actually call that broken-down doctor over here at three o'clock in the morning?

LANG: Yes, I did. And I'm going to keep calling him until you stop snoring.

DON: Do you know what that quack charges? You made seven visits to his offices last month and he charged you five dollars every time he looked at your tongue!

LANG: What about it?

DON: Just think how much you could save if you'd keep your mouth shut!

LANG: For your information I'm going to make seven more visits next month.

DON: Blanche, I can't afford those bills! What in the world are you thinking of?

LANG: Nothing.

DON: Well, take your mind off yourself. Goodnight.

LANG: Just let me get sick one day and you resent it. A lot you care that I walk around half-dead. I've got a terrible sinking sensation—and my liver's run-down.

DON: Wind it up and go to sleep.

LANG: That's right—make light of it.

DON: Put out the light.

LANG: Don't you talk to me like that, John Bickerson!

DON: Oh, dear.

LANG: If you'd have talked like that when you first met me I never would have married you.

DON: Now she tells me.

LANG: You make it sound like I got the bargain. What have I got to show for my marriage? A home? No. Servants? No. Jewels? No. Housemaids' knee and dishwater hands. That's all I've got.

DON: Here we go.

LANG: All you do is treat me like a slave. Just use me—make sure I press your pants twice a week. One day you'll find out your wife is more important than your pants.

DON: Oh, I don't know—there's lots of places I can go without my wife.

LANG: I don't doubt that at all. And you've probably been going there.

DON: Going where?

LANG: The signs are plain enough, John. Your mind isn't on me. I suppose you know when you finished breakfast this morning you left me a fifty-cent tip.

DON: What about it? You know very well I eat my lunch in a restaurant—it's just a force of habit.

LANG: That's just it.

DON: What's just it?

LANG: When I helped you on with your coat you kissed me!

DON: I always kiss you before I go to work in the morning.

LANG: Why?

DON: Why?

LANG: Yes, why? You don't love me. Why don't you admit it?

DON: Because it's not true.

LANG: I can see how you act. And it'll only get worse. You'll love me less and less as the years go by.

DON: I will not!

LANG: You will, too!

DON: I swear I couldn't love you any less than I do now! Now you know that's not what I meant to say!

LANG: Well, if you'd only stop to think before you start yelling maybe we wouldn't fight so much.

DON: I'd never yell if you didn't goad me.

LANG: I don't do it purposely, John. It's just that I never feel sure about your love. Not enough husbands take marriage seriously these days.

DON: I do, brother.

LANG: Only yesterday I read where a farmer actually traded his wife for an old plow horse. You wouldn't do that, would you, John?

DON: Do what?

LANG: Trade me for an old plow horse.

DON: No—but I'd hate anybody to tempt me with a new Cadillac. Why don't you go to sleep, Blanche?

LANG: Tell me the truth, John—if anything happened to me—would you marry again?

DON: Never! I hope my nose drops off if I ever marry again.
LANG: Well, you don't have to sound so violent.
DON: I can't convince you any other way. I take an oath, Blanche, I wouldn't wipe my feet on the best woman in the world, except you! Does that satisfy you?
LANG: I guess so.
DON: Goodnight.
LANG: Goodnight…John.
DON: Mmm.
LANG: Will you do me a favor in the morning?
DON: Mmm.
LANG: I have an eight o'clock appointment at the beauty parlor and I wish you'd stop at the butcher shop for me. I want three lamb chops and a quarter-pound of hog liver.
DON: Hog liver?
LANG: I know you hate lamb chops. Be sure you go to Floyd's butcher shop on the corner. He always gives me the best cuts of meat.
DON: Okay.
LANG: And don't tell the butcher you're my husband—he doesn't know I'm married.
DON: What! What kind of business is that? You spend all my money in the beauty parlor to look pretty for the butcher!
LANG: It isn't easy to get good meat these days.
DON: What's good about hog liver? A hog won't even eat it!
LANG: I don't care. You never give me any compliments so I get them from the butcher. He thinks I have a very trim figure.
DON: Well, why doesn't he trim some of it?
LANG: You're just jealous! It's a funny thing you never complain about that big balloon, Gloria Gooseby!
DON: Now don't start with Gloria Gooseby!
LANG: If you were her poor husband you'd never be able to get your arms around her waist.
DON: I'm not her husband and I always get my arms around her waist! I mean, I wouldn't touch Gloria Gooseby with a barge pole—and I never want you to mention her name again! Do you hear me?

LANG: Oh, hush up and go to sleep.

DON: Go to sleep she says...Steams me up with Gloria Gooseby...gets hog liver in a beauty parlor...Drives me crazy with butchers...now she tells me to go to sleep. I'll—never—sleep—another—wink as long—as I—(SNORES...PAUSE...PHONE RINGS)

LANG: John!

DON: Mmm.

LANG: The telephone. Answer it.

DON: Hello.

LANG: Go to the phone and answer it.

DON: Oh. (STUMBLES OUT OF BED) Who can be calling at this time of—(CRASHES INTO NIGHT TABLE) Owwww! (RECEIVER UP) Hello.

MAN: (FILTER) Mr. Bickerson?

DON: Yes?

MAN: This is Mr. Hooker. I live on the floor above you. Been living above you for seven years. Did you know that?

DON: No—and I could have stood the suspense another five hours.

MAN: The fact is, your horrible snoring tears my head off every night and I've been lying awake for seven years trying to think of a way to help you. I've finally concluded the trouble lies in your throat, and I've got just the thing for it.

DON: What is it?

MAN: A stout rope. Shall I drop down?

DON: No—DROP DEAD! (SLAMS RECEIVER) I never heard of such a thing! (GETS BACK IN BED) I'm gonna move out of here first chance I get.

LANG: John.

DON: Mmm.

LANG: Are you angry with me?

DON: No. I'm just sleepy.

LANG: Wouldn't you like to kiss me goodnight?

DON: I'll kiss you goodnight in the morning.

LANG: Why can't you kiss me now?

DON: I'm not facing that way. Goodnight, Blanche.

LANG: John, I have something important to tell you.

DON: Mmm.

LANG: Do you realize I'm the only woman in my set who doesn't have an engagement ring?

DON: You have, too! I gave you a beautiful ring—fourteen-carat gold-filled—and it had an enormous hole in the top for a diamond.

LANG: I bought a diamond ring for three hundred dollars.

DON: Blanche! You didn't!

LANG: I had to! After living with you for seven years I was ashamed to face my friends. They were starting to talk.

DON: About what?

LANG: About us. Everybody knows we're not legally engaged.

DON: Blanche! Have you gone out of your mind? How can you squander three hundred dollars on a diamond ring?

LANG: Don't scream at me!

DON: I deny myself everything! I've been cutting down your old girdles and wearing 'em for suspenders—I've been using chicken fat for moustache wax—my only bathing suit has a hole in the knee! I haven't spent a nickel on myself for six years and she buys diamonds!

LANG: You had a new lining put in your coat last week.

DON: That wasn't a new lining! It was a patch to hold the shoulders together! Where's that ring, Blanche? Lemme see it.

LANG: Here.

DON: There's no diamond in this ring! It's the same one I bought you!

LANG: I didn't buy anything, silly! Why would I spend three hundred dollars on a diamond ring when we haven't got enough to eat? Who am I going to fool? My friends know we're paupers.

DON: Oh, they do, huh?

LANG: Certainly. They laugh up their sleeve every time they see me wear that ring with the hole in it.

DON: Is that so? Well, I'll put a stop to that, honey. I'll take it to the jeweller's in the morning.

LANG: John! Are you going to put a diamond in it?

DON: No, I'm gonna plug up the hole. Goodnight, Blanche.

LANG:	Goodnight, John.
MUSIC:	BICKERSON PLAYOFF
	(APPLAUSE)
MUSIC:	THEME
AMECHE:	Well, that puts the lid on the eighteenth program of our new series for Old Gold Cigarettes, written and directed by Phil Rapp and produced by Mann Holiner.
	And, say, did you know that that snappy Marine Corps uniform is being worn by civilians these days—civilians who are members of the new Citizen Marine Corps. Their membership is purely voluntary. They share the pride and prestige of the nation's proudest military organization. They benefit themselves and help guarantee peace for America by being in the Citizen Marine Corps. And, they can earn while they learn, as Civilian Marines. Any Marine Corps activity center has the details.
	Well, we hope you'll be on hand next Friday night for Frank Morgan, Frances Langford, and Carmen Dragon and the orchestra. This is Don Ameche saying goodnight and good smoking with Old Golds!
	(APPLAUSE)
MUSIC:	(THEME)
MILLER:	Frank Morgan appeared by arrangement with Metro-Goldwyn-Mayer—producers of Sinclair Lewis' "Cass Timberlane" starring Spencer Tracy, Lana Turner, and Zachary Scott.
	Remember next Friday at Old Gold Time it'll be Frank Morgan, Don Ameche, and Frances Langford with Carmen Dragon and his orchestra brought to you by P. Lorillard Company…a famous name in tobaccos for nearly two hundred years…makers of Old Gold Cigarettes…the treasure of 'em all…treat yourself to Old Golds. Buy 'em at your tobacco counters…Buy them in the cigarette vending machines…
	Don't forget every Friday night on C.B.S. it's "Fun For The Family." Stay tuned now for "The Adventures of Ozzie and Harriet" which follows immediately over most of these stations. This is Marvin Miller speaking.
	(APPLAUSE)
	This is…CBS…THE COLUMBIA BROADCASTING SYSTEM… (Don Ameche, co-starred with Claudette Colbert, will soon be seen in their new picture "Sleep My Love.")

THE OLD GOLD SHOW MARCH 19, 1948

MUSIC: (ON CUE) OPENING FANFARE

MILLER: (ON CUE) From Hollywood.

CHORUS: (ON CUE) It's Old Gold Cigarette Time.
If you want a treat instead of a treatment
Smoke Old Golds.
If you want a treat instead of a treatment
Smoke Old Golds
We're tobacco men, not medicine men
Pleasure is what we pack
Oh, Old Gold cures just one thing
The world's best tobacco!
So, it you want a treat instead of a treatment
If you want a treat instead of a treatment
Smoke, smoke, smoke, smoke—Smoke Old Gold

(PAUSE)

MARVIN: The treasure of 'em all, gives the most pleasure of 'em all

MUSIC: THEME...(ESTABLISH AND FADE UNDER FOLLOWING)

MILLER: This is Marvin Miller, Ladies and Gentlemen, speaking for the makers of Old Gold Cigarettes who are pleased to present the twenty-sixth in a series of new programs with Carmen Dragon and his orchestra, starring Metro-Goldwyn-Mayer's lovable Frank Morgan, the genial Don Ameche and charming Frances Langford, who sings—

MUSIC: LANGFORD AND ORCH..."AIN'T MISBEHAVIN'"

FIRST COMMERCIAL

MILLER: We're tobacco men...not medicine men. Old Gold cures just one thing...the world's best tobacco. And the one thing we sell is...tobacco pleasure...pleasure...as real and solid as the Old Gold you put between your lips. After all...nearly two hundred years of quality tobacco experience are behind every Old Gold you smoke. And friends...you simply cannot match the finer taste...the smooth...mild pleasure of an Old Gold.

CHORUS: So...if you want a treat instead of a treatment
If you want a treat instead of a treatment
Smoke, smoke, smoke, smoke
Smoke...Old Golds.

MILLER: Now here is your host for the evening, Don Ameche.

(APPLAUSE)

AMECHE: Thank you, ladies and gentlemen, and good evening. For several weeks now, I've been interrupted by our orchestra leader, Carmen Dragon, with a request to tell a joke. And so tonight, before we bring on our guest, I'd like to introduce Mr. Dragon with his joke. Carmen.

DRAG: Hey, what do you think you're doing, hey?

AMECHE: You know what I'm doing, hey. You want to tell a joke, don't you?

DRAG: No, I don't!

AMECHE: No?

DRAG: No—N-O-E—no! I'm not wasting anymore of my yockers to make you a big-shot with the sponsor, boy.

AMECHE: Carmen, what are you talking about?

DRAG: Never mind, boy. You know what I mean, boy.

AMECHE: What do you mean, boy? I always help you with your jokes, don't I?

DRAG: Sure. Every time you help me with a joke I sound like an idiot—and I don't need your help for that.

LANG: Oh, go on, Carmen—tell your joke.

DRAG: Not unless Don asks me. I happen to have a great yocker, too.

AMECHE: All right—tell your yocker.

DRAG: Okay. Two bald-headed rabbits got married and are expecting a little hare in the spring. Like it?

AMECHE: Hate it! Now do you mind if I introduce our guest?

DRAG: If I minded would it make any difference?

AMECHE: No. Ladies and gentlemen, in keeping with our policy of presenting outstanding people in every profession, I'd like you to meet Steve Reeves, the greatest male physical specimen in the United States—present holder of the most coveted title among the muscle men—Mr. America in person! Here he is!

(APPLAUSE)

REEVES: Thank you.

AMECHE: Steve, since this isn't television it's only fair that we give the listening audience an idea of what you look like. To begin with—how tall are you?

REEVES:	Six feet one.
AMECHE:	Weight?
REEVES:	Two hundred and ten.
AMECHE:	Chest?
REEVES:	Fifty-one inches, expanded.
AMECHE:	Neck?
REEVES:	When I get the chance.
AMECHE:	No, no, I meant the measurement.
REEVES:	Oh, seventeen and a half.
AMECHE:	What do you think of him, Frances?
LANG:	Pretty good, I say. You have a wonderful figure, Mr. Reeves.
REEVES:	Yours isn't so bad, either, Miss Langford.
DRAG:	How do you like that? His eyes are bulging more than his muscles.
AMECHE:	Never mind, Carmen. Steve, just for the record—how old are you?
REEVES:	I'm twenty-one.
LANG:	Only twenty-one? When did you start your body-building exercise?
REEVES:	Not until I was seventeen. I was a horrible physical wreck, with a shape like a sack of potatoes. What do you think brought about this change?
AMECHE:	What change?
DRAG:	Oh, he's starting again. Never mind, boy. I'll bet I can lift heavier weights than this guy here.
REEVES:	I don't go in for weight-lifting, Mr. Dragon. I built myself up with a variety of exercises.
AMECHE:	Since when do you lift weights, Carmen?
DRAG:	I've been taking a health course for the last nine weeks.
LANG:	You have?
DRAG:	Sure. When I first started I could hardly lift a sixty-pound weight. Saturday night I went to the gym, and what do you think?
AMECHE:	What?
DRAG:	I stripped down to my shorts and picked up a two hundred pound dumbbell.

MORG:	(COMING ON) You did? Well, see if she can get a friend for me. I'll bring my own shorts.
AMECHE:	Frank!
	(APPLAUSE)
MORG:	As long as she's dumb I don't care what she weighs. When can I get a look at this chunky cherub, Herman?
AMECHE:	Frank—what are you talking about?
MORG:	I don't know—what are you talking about?
AMECHE:	Lifting weights—not women!
MORG:	Oh, woman's waist. Uplift. Well, why didn't somebody—I'll be glad to—(TAKES ANOTHER LOOK) Dodger, who's that skinny-looking fink standing behind you?
REEVES:	Do you mean me, Mr. Morgan?
MORG:	I mean you, Mr. Fink! You don't fool me for a minute. I've seen those suits with the built-in muscles before. When you take off your jacket the shoulders stay inside.
LANG:	Mr. Morgan, please! Mr. Reeves is here to demonstrate how to build a beautiful body.
MORG:	Well, let him build one for me, size thirty-size, blonde, with—Oh, hello, my dear!
LANG:	Hello.
MORG:	Well! I had no idea you were interested in physical culture. If you'll run down to my Athletic Club I'll be glad to build up your physique and tear down your resistance. Good for your health.
LANG:	Well, I'll tell my husband…
MORG:	No, that'll be bad for my health. Let's consider it settled. I'll expect you tomorrow at 9 a.m. dressed for gym.
LANG:	Dressed for gym?
MORG:	Yes, after Jim goes home you can change your dress. How much do you weigh, my dear?
LANG:	A hundred and fourteen pounds.
MORG:	Only a hundred and fourteen pounds. But you make every pound count. I wish you'd stop wiggling so I could count 'em.
LANG:	That's enough for me. Goodnight, gentlemen. (SHE GOES)
MORG:	(LOOKING AFTER HER) A beautiful blossom. With her figure

	and my brains we could make a fortune out of Physical Culture.
AMECHE:	With her figure and your brains?
MORG:	Yes. She has such a well-trained carriage and I've got such a one-track mind. Well, I guess I'll be—
AMECHE:	Just a minute, Frank. What's this about you running a Health School. Is this something new?
MORG:	New? There are countless adherents to the Morgan Health System.
REEVES:	Morgan Health System?
MORG:	Yes. My pupils are legion—and you must have heard the slogan that's been echoed by a million voices—"To Health with Morgan!"
AMECHE:	Uh-huh. Well, you should get along fine with this gentleman. He's interested in physical culture.
REEVES:	That's right, Mr. Morgan.
MORG:	Well, he's too far gone, Dodger. You can't make a silk purse out of a sow's ear, you know. You'd better see a blood donor, lad.
REEVES:	I beg your pardon?
MARG:	You're too flabby, son. Your pectoral muscles dangle like a bunch of grapes and your chest is slung lower than a new Hudson. However, three treatments from the Morgan Health System and you'll have a chest as big as mine.
AMECHE:	Listen, Morgan—does the title "Mr. America" mean anything to you?
MORG:	Naturally, my boy. It means everything to me and I'm proud to have won it.
AMECHE:	What!
MORG:	The contest took place in June of last year and my closest opponent had the build of an ox.
REEVES:	Who was he?
MORG:	An ox. But he never had a chance. I was in prime condition and my horns were longer. I was a perfect specimen—a hundred and ninety pounds of solid fat, not an ounce of muscle. The judges were unanimous in their decision.
REEVES:	Excuse me, Mr. Morgan—but I thought that Steve Reeves was voted Mr. America last year.
MORG:	He was! But he was disqualified for cheating in the weight-lifting test.

AMECHE: Cheating? How?

MORG: He had a derrick concealed in his undershirt. Poor fellow, left the arena like a whipped cur, with his lumbar extensor dragging.

REEVES: This comes as quite a shock to me, Mr. Morgan.

MORG: It wouldn't surprise you if you knew the thief. Do you know him?

REEVES: I am him.

MORG: You am? I mean—you are?

AMECHE: Yes, Morgan—this is the famous Mr. America, Steve Reeves.

MORG: Oh, Famous American sneak-thief. Well—

AMECHE: Well, nothing! I insist that you apologize to Mr. Reeves for all those lies.

MORG: Nonsense! In order to prove my claims I'm perfectly willing to enter into a contest of strength with Mr. Sneak.

REEVES: Reeves.

MORG: Yes. You can exhibit your strength in anyway you like, and I'll go you one better.

REEVES: Well, I really don't want to—

AMECHE: Go on—please, Steve.

REEVES: All right. Fetch me a telephone book.

MORG: What are you going to do with a telephone book?

REEVES: I'm going to tear it in half.

MORG: Oh...dodger—fetch me a telephone operator!

AMECHE: A telephone operator?

MORG: I may not tear her in half—but I can probably disconnect her.

AMECHE: Go on! You couldn't rip through a piece of wet Kleenex with a bolo knife buckled to your nose.

MORG: What!

AMECHE: You heard me. Only a fat-headed hillbilly from the mountains would believe you.

MILLER: I don't want to intrude, Don—but I believe Mr. Morgan.

MORG: Well! It's that fat young hillbilly from the mountains. Pull up a mountain and rest your fat hill, Billy.

AMECHE: Now don't start that again, Morgan. There's nothing wrong with Marvin's physique.

MORG: Who said there was? Why, his body could win him the title of Mr. U.S.A.

MILLER: Mr. Morgan, I'd like to ask you—

AMECHE: Marvin, I won't have you falling for his hogwash every week! He doesn't know anything about Physical Culture!

MORG: Poppycock! The Morgans have been body-builders for generations. Beginning with my grandfather Horizontal Bar Morgan, down to my Uncle Springboard and my Aunt Trapeze.

AMECHE: Your Aunt Trapeze?

MORG: A stringy old thing. Always hung from the rafters when she was swinging.

MILLER: What a wonderful family.

MORG: Yes. Under their tutelage I mastered the nine laws of exercise for health.

AMECHE: Let's hear the nine laws for health, Morgan.

MORG: To begin with, early and rapid rising is the first requirement. It has long been a part of my health regime to rise promptly at dawn, take a brisk, ice-cold bottle of beer and go to sleep again.

AMECHE: If that's the first law, I don't want to hear the other eight.

MORG: Skepticism is the true mark of the dolt, Dodger. It might interest you to know that at the age of twelve I startled the American Society of Athletics when I demonstrated my new method for strengthening my muscles by constantly bouncing my back on a hard waitress. Mattress!

MILLER: You meant to say mattress, of course.

AMECHE: Of course.

MORG: Of course.

MILLER: Of course.

AMECHE: Oh, I've had enough of this! Morgan, if you do all this strong-man stuff why is it you always look like you're about to fall down?

MORG: Well, I'm over-trained. And besides, lately I've developed a bad case of Playboy's Rheumatism.

AMECHE: Playboy's Rheumatism?

MORG: Yes, I keep getting stiff in the joints.

AMECHE: Frank—how much did you say your chest measured?

MORG:	Sixty-four inches. If I had a tape-measure I could prove to your satisfaction that—
REEVES:	I have a tape-measure.
MORG:	Well, I don't think it's necessary to—
AMECHE:	No, you don't! Come on, Morgan—we've got a tape-measure—start expanding your chest.
MORG:	Not now, Dodger. I'm tried and I don't want to strain my lungs.
AMECHE:	Strain your lungs?
MORG:	Yes, I've been breathing with them all day. Maybe another time—
AMECHE:	Come back here—hold him, Steve!...Now let me get this tape-measure around you.
MORG:	Oh, all right.
AMECHE:	Let's see...Well, I'll be darned! It's sixty-four inches.
MORG:	That's nothing. Wait 'till I expand it. (TAKES A DEEP BREATH)
AMECHE:	Hold it.
REEVES:	What does it measure now?
AMECHE:	Thirty-two and a half.
MORG:	What?
AMECHE:	What happened, Frank? How come your chest measures less when it's expanded?
MORG:	I don't know—I must have developed a slow leak. So long, fellows, I gotta buy a bicycle pump.
MUSIC:	MORG PLAYOFF
	SECOND COMMERCIAL
MUSIC:	INTRO "NOW IS THE HOUR"
MILLER:	(OVER THEME) Frances Langford sings "Now Is The Hour."
MUSIC:	ORCH AND LANGFORD..."NOW IS THE HOUR"
	(APPLAUSE)
CHORUS:	If you want a treat instead of a treatment Smoke Old Golds If you want a treat instead of a treatment Smoke Old Golds

MILLER: Friends, our little choral group here is singing to no one else but you. Yes...give yourself a treat—in the cigarette that can't be matched for smooth mildness and wonderful taste, Old Golds. Yes—Old Gold, the treasure of 'em all...with a quality tobacco tradition unmatched by any other cigarette. You know—nearly two hundred years of fine tobacco experience and knowledge are back of Old Golds—helping us bring you, in every Old Gold, the ripest, mellowest, best-tasting tobacco a cigarette can hold. That's something real...something you taste and enjoy when you smoke an Old Golds. And that's the whole point. Listen—

2ND ANNCR: We're tobacco men—not medicine men. Old Golds cures just one thing...the world's best tobacco.

(SECOND COMMERCIAL CONT'D)

MILLER: That's right. Fine, choice, ripe tobaccos—that make Old Golds so much smoother and mellower, so much tastier and more pleasing. Tonight or tomorrow morning, get a pack of Old Golds. Then, as you smoke them compare the downright enjoyment an Old Gold gives you with anything else you ever smoked. Do—just—exactly—that, won't you.

CHORUS: SO...if you want a treat instead of a treatment
If you want a treat instead of a treatment
Smoke, smoke, smoke, smoke
Smoke, Old Golds.

MILLER: Now here is Don Ameche and Frances Langford as John and Blanche Bickerson in "The Honeymoon is Over"

THEME: (SOFT AND PLAINTIVE)

MILLER: It is two o'clock in the morning and Mrs. Bickerson has just returned from an out-of-town visit to her mother. After waiting vainly at the station for husband John to pick her up, Blanche Bickerson arrives at the apartment, finds herself without a doorkey, and is forced to rouse the janitor to let her in. Listen.

LANG: I'm sorry I had to wake you up, Mr. Homer, but I knocked and knocked and I guess Mr. Bickerson isn't in. He must have gone to the wrong station.

MAN: (JINGLES A LOT OF KEYS) Should carry an extra key.

LANG: I usually do, but when I changed purses I forgot to take it out. John used to leave an extra key in the letterbox.

MAN: Maybe it's still there...Let's have a look. Hmmm.

LANG: Is there anything in there?

MAN: Just half a bottle of bourbon. Better take it with you. (JINGLES KEY...KEY IN DOOR...DOOR OPENS) There you are.

DON: (SNORES LUSTILY...WHINES)

MAN: I thought I fixed that radiator.

LANG: That's my husband!

DON: (SNORES)

MAN: Is he strangling?

DON: (WHINES)

LANG: No, he snores like that. Thanks very much—goodnight.

(DOOR CLOSES)

DON: (SNORES AND GIGGLES MERRILY)

LANG: John! John!

DON: (A PROTESTING WHINE) Mmmmmmmmmmmm!

LANG: Stop it, stop it, stop it!

DON: Stop it, Blanche. Wassamatter? What time is it, Blanche?

LANG: This is the last straw, John Bickerson! I waited down at that station for over an hour and I come home to find you snoring!

DON: Snoring.

LANG: How can you have the brass to sleep like that while I pound the door until my knuckles are blue? What'll you try on me next?

DON: Brass knuckles.

LANG: Sit up and stop being so funny! Sit up, John!

DON: What happened? What time is it? What're you doing home so early?

LANG: Why didn't you meet me at the station?

DON: It isn't time yet. You said you'd get in at one-thirty and it isn't even near that! Look at the clock.

LANG: John Bickerson! Daylight Saving's been on for a whole week and you haven't changed the clock yet!

DON: I have, too! I set it back an hour last Sunday! I've been working overtime and they've been docking my salary.

LANG: I had to wake the janitor to let me in. I was never so embarrassed in all my life. He opened the letterbox to look for the extra key and found this bourbon.

DON:	What bourbon?
LANG:	Here. What was it doing in the letterbox?
DON:	I put it there.
LANG:	What for?
DON:	That's my emergency rations in case I get locked out.
LANG:	That's all you ever think about—bourbon! I'm sure you never gave me a single thought all the time I was gone.
DON:	Oh, I did, too!
LANG:	Then why didn't you meet me at the station?
DON:	I told you, Blanche—my clock was set wrong!
LANG:	I'll bet you did it on purpose!
DON:	Will you please get undressed and go to bed?
LANG:	No. I wish I hadn't come home. I almost didn't, anyway.
DON:	What?
LANG:	When you didn't answer the phone I was going to call the Shaws to put me up for the night.
DON:	How could the Shaws put you up? They live in a piano crate.
LANG:	They do not. They've got a very nice penthouse on top of the United Nations pool hall.
DON:	Penthouse.
LANG:	Yes, and if they didn't have room for me Louise has something in the apartment hotel next door.
DON:	Louise has nothing in that apartment hotel. It's all rented.
LANG:	It is not. I know for a fact that Louise Shaw has a bachelor on the second floor.
DON:	Does her husband know about it?
LANG:	I'm talking about a bachelor apartment. I wish we could live there. It's a beautiful place and I'm sick of this rat's nest.
DON:	Nothing wrong with this rat's nest.
LANG:	You'd move in that hotel quick enough if Gloria Gooseby lived there.
DON:	Now don't start with Gloria Gooseby!
LANG:	If you were closer to her it would be easier for you to see your secret love.

DON: I'm always close to her and it's no secret! I mean, I hate the sight of Gloria Gooseby!

LANG: I swear I don't know what you see in that woman.

DON: I don't see anything in her.

LANG: She may have a pretty face and a nice figure—but I've got brains, and after all it's the little things that count.

DON: Why don't you let me sleep, Blanche? I don't wanna fight anymore.

LANG: John.

DON: Mmm.

LANG: Are you sorry I came home?

DON: You know I am, Blanche.

LANG: What?

DON: I mean no!

LANG: Did you miss me?

DON: Yes.

LANG: I don't believe it. You never missed me for a minute.

DON: I tell you I did!

LANG: Well, say it!

DON: I missed you for a minute. Now please put out the lights and let me get some sleep.

LANG: I won't. Not until you tell me how much you missed me. Every woman's got a right to be missed.

DON: Blanche, I missed you in the morning, I missed you in the afternoon, I missed you at night—I wish you hadn't come home so I could miss you some more.

LANG: Nobody knows how I suffer. Go away for a week and come home to have you scream at me.

DON: I'm not screaming.

LANG: And how do you greet me? No kiss, no hug—just a long snore.

DON: Oh, dear.

LANG: I don't understand you. I swear I don't, John. How can you be so unaffectionate? I'd rather die than be so cold and heartless.

DON: Listen, you'd better not talk. The only time you're affectionate is when you want money.

LANG:	Well, isn't that often enough?
DON:	You can say that again.
LANG:	It's easy for you to talk now. Before we were married you sang a different song.
DON:	Yeah.
LANG:	I was foolish enough to fall for your line. None of the other girls would even look at you. You squandered your money on them—you bought them presents—they took you for everything. And what did you get out of them—nothing!
DON:	Oh, I don't know about that. No woman ever made a fool out of me.
LANG:	Well, who did it then?
DON:	What kind of a crack is that?
LANG:	Well, if you had any brains you'd treat me with a little more consideration. You might at least ask me how I enjoyed my trip.
DON:	I'll ask you in the morning.
LANG:	You knew my mother wasn't feeling too well—it wouldn't hurt you to ask how she is.
DON:	How is she?
LANG:	What do you care!
DON:	I don't—I'm just trying to be polite.
LANG:	Well, you needn't try. In all the years we've been married you've never cared about a single member of my family.
DON:	How can you say that, Blanche! Not a day goes by that I don't inquire the state of your rich uncle's health!
LANG:	Well, I don't like the way you inquire.
DON:	What do you mean?
LANG:	It isn't nice to keep asking "Is the old goat dead yet?"
DON:	Well, is he?
LANG:	No—and if you think you're going to get any of his money you've got another guess coming. He's made a new will and everything goes to my family.
DON:	It does, huh? Well, I hope he lives to be a thousand!
LANG:	John! How can you wish such a terrible thing on my family!

DON: Listen, Blanche, I have to get up in the morning and go to work. Will you please put out the lights and let me get some rest?

LANG: I will as soon as I've checked everything. I suppose you left a stack of dirty dishes in the sink.

DON: No dishes.

LANG: Were the animals fed regularly?

DON: Every day.

LANG: Did you put fresh sand in the cat's bed.

DON: Mmm.

LANG: The water in the goldfish bowl should have been changed on Wednesday.

DON: I changed it. I cleaned up everything.

LANG: How's the canary?

DON: I don't know. I haven't seen him since I vacuumed his cage.

LANG: John Bickerson!

DON: Oh, don't blow you top! The canary's fine!

LANG: Did you give him his bath?

DON: I gave him his bath, I powdered his tail and I plucked his eyebrows! What do you want from me, Blanche?

LANG: I'll bet you didn't let the cat out tonight.

DON: Yes, I did!

LANG: You're sure you're not lying, John?

DON: Well, if you think I'm lying go let him out yourself! I'm sick of playing nursemaid to a broken-down alley cat!

LANG: He's a beautiful cat and I love him.

DON: I hate him.

LANG: You wouldn't feel that way if you got a little friendly with him. It's easy to make up to a cat.

DON: Mmm.

LANG: Why don't you bring him something to play with?

DON: I'll bring him a dog in the morning. Goodnight.

LANG: I suppose I'll have to get some groceries tomorrow. Is there any milk for breakfast?

DON: No.
LANG: Then you'll have to eat out.
DON: I don't care. I've been doing it all week.
LANG: What for? I left you enough food for six days. I cooked a whole bathtub of rice. What happened to it?
DON: I took a bath in it.
LANG: Why didn't you eat it?
DON: I've told you a million times I can't stand the sight of rice.
LANG: Why not?
DON: Because it's connected with one of the saddest mistakes of my life!
LANG: Oh, that's too bad about you. I suppose you think I got a bargain?
DON: I don't think anything—I'm just sleepy.
LANG: Well, you'd just better start waking up to a few things, John. You don't know what the future has in store for you.
DON: Neither do you.
LANG: You'd be surprised. I didn't go to a fortune teller for nothing, you know.
DON: When did you go to a fortune teller?
LANG: Last Monday. I've always wanted to know exactly where I'm going to die.
DON: What's the good of knowing that?
LANG: What's the good? If I know where I'm going to die I'll never go near the place.
DON: I never heard of such an idiotic thing in all my life! Do you mean to tell me you believe in that stuff, Blanche?
LANG: Certainly. This fortune teller told me plenty of things that all came true.
DON: Like what?
LANG: Well, for one thing she told me I was going to buy some stock. That's pretty good, isn't it, John?
DON: No, it isn't. The market's going to pieces.
LANG: Well, I got a piece of it.
DON: Blanche! You didn't throw any of my money into the stock market!
LANG: I cashed in our government bonds and bought three hundred shares of Seersucker Aviation.

DON: Seersucker Aviation!

LANG: I think they make sleeper planes. A lot of people told me it's a fly by night investment.

DON: Ohhh! Take it back! Take it back, you hear me!

LANG: Don't get so hysterical!

DON: How can you do this to me? You've squandered my life's savings! I deny myself everything! I learned how to bark so I could get free lunches at the dog pound—yesterday I sold my fillings to pay my dentist bills! I can't even afford to buy a pair of pants—I wear a long jacket and walk on my knees! I never spend a penny on myself!

LANG: You had your shoes shined last Sunday.

DON: I haven't got any shoes—I had my feet painted black! You go down to the stock market and get my money back, Blanche.

LANG: Oh, stop carrying on like a lunatic.

DON: How can I help it! All you ever do is spend, spend, spend!

LANG: I'll sell the stock first thing in the morning. We won't lose anything on it.

DON: Ohhhh. How can a woman upset a man constantly like that?

LANG: I guess I wouldn't do these silly things if I had something to occupy my mind. Maybe I ought to get a job.

DON: Forget it.

LANG: It wouldn't be so bad if I had a baby to take care of or something. I get so lonesome during the day—and you don't seem to love me any more.

DON: I love you.

LANG: You used to kiss me goodnight and let me tuck you in bed like a baby—you don't anymore.

DON: Go to sleep, Blanche.

LANG: John, would you mind if I just tucked you in bed tonight?

DON: Okay—tuck me in bed.

LANG: All right, dear. Lift your head so I can straighten the pillow…Stretch your feet out…Now, let me get these covers under…There. All tucked in.

DON: Thanks.

LANG: Are you comfortable?

DON:	Perfectly.
LANG:	Are you sure?
DON:	Never felt more comfortable in my life.
LANG:	Fine. Now you get up and tuck me in.
DON:	Goodnight, Blanche.
LANG:	Goodnight, John.
MUSIC:	BICKERSON PLAYOFF
	APPLAUSE
MUSIC:	THEME
	CLOSING
AMECHE:	Well, that puts the lid on the twenty-sixth program of our new series for Old Gold Cigarettes, written and directed by Phil Rapp. We hope you'll be on hand next Friday night for Frank Morgan, Frances Langford, and Carmen Dragon and the orchestra. This is Don Ameche saying goodnight and good smoking with Old Gold.
	(APPLAUSE)
MUSIC:	THEME
MILLER:	Frank Morgan appeared by arrangement with Metro-Goldwyn-Mayer, producers of "The Bride Goes Wild," starring Van Johnson, June Allyson and "Butch" Jenkins. Remember next Friday at Old Gold Time it'll be Frank Morgan, Don Ameche, and Frances Langford with Carmen Dragon and his orchestra brought to you by P. Lorrillard Company…a famous name in tobaccos for nearly two hundred years…makers of Old Gold Cigarettes…the treasure of 'em all…and listen…if you want a treat instead of a treatment…treat yourself to Old Golds…Buy 'em at your tobacco counters…Buy them in the cigarette vending machines. Don't forget every Friday night on CBS it's "Fun For The Family." Stay tuned now for "The Adventures of Ozzie and Harriet," which follows immediately over most of these stations. This is Marvin Miller speaking.
	(APPLAUSE)
	THIS IS CBS…THE COLUMBIA BROADCASTING SYSTEM…
	(Don Ameche co-starred with Claudette Colbert, can now be seen in their new picture, "Sleep My Love.")
	CLOSING

THE CHARLIE MCCARTHY SHOW

	(AFTER COMMERCIAL)
CHARLIE:	Say, Ken...
CARP:	Yes, Charlie?
CHARLIE:	I hope my next door neighbors were listening to you tonight.
CARP:	Why? Are they early morning grouches?
CHARLIE:	Early morning—late at night—these people fight all the time. I call 'em the Bickering Bickersons.
CARP:	Have they been keeping you up, Charlie?
CHARLIE:	Well, last night I had my first good night's sleep because they went out of town. Mrs. Bickerson received a wire telling her that she was mentioned in her Uncle's will, so she and her husband went up to his house to find out how much they collected. I'll bet wherever they are (FADING) they're arguing...
MUSIC:	(THEME...THEN FADE OUT)
	(FOOTSTEPS WALKING)
MAR:	Here's our room, John...(DOOR OPENS) It used to be Uncle Thurmond's.
DON:	Uncle Thurmond.
MAR:	There was only one bed in it, so I had them bring in a cot.
DON:	Mmm.
MAR:	Of course, it's only an old army cot, but I think it'll do for the night, don't you, John?
DON:	It'll do fine. 'Night, Blanche. (CREAKING OF BEDSPRINGS)
MAR:	John!
DON:	Mmmm?
MAR:	The cot's over here.
DON:	What about it?

61

MAR: What about it? How can you sleep in that comfortable bed while I sit up half the night in this tacky army cot?

DON: It won't be easy, Blanche. Put out the light.

MAR: I'll do nothing of the sort. I won't put out the light till you promise to change places with me.

DON: I promise.

MAR: We'll take turns sleeping in it. Fifty-fifty.

DON: Okay. I'll sleep in it tonight and you can have it in the morning.

MAR: I want it right now. Get up, John.

DON: Please, Blanche! You won't like it—it's got a big lump in the middle.

MAR: What kind of a lump?

DON: I don't know. I think it's your Uncle Thurmond.

MAR: John Bickerson! How can you say such a thing?

DON: I'm sorry, Blanche...I'm so sleepy, I don't know what I'm saying. You had no right to drag me down here to listen to your Uncle Thurmond's will. You know I have to get up so early in the morning.

MAR: Well, how did I know what was going to happen?

DON: "Wait till they read my Uncle's will," she tells me. "You won't have to work any more," she says. "We'll have ten servants and you'll bathe in bourbon," she promised. "I'll buy you a new toothbrush and you can throw away that sawed-off whiskbroom you've been using." Promises, that's all, promises.

MAR: John—

DON: And what did that fabulously wealthy Uncle of yours leave you? Two-hundred-and-fifty-thousand calendars with Honest John's picture on them. And they're all dated 1943.

MAR: Well, they're worth something. We can sell them.

DON: Sure. If 1943 ever comes back you'll make a fortune. Put out the lights, Blanche.

MAR: I will as soon as I get my things off. You know, none of the other relatives did very well, either. Clara's husband, Barney, was so disappointed.

DON: What did he get?

MAR: Two cases of ping-pong balls and a season pass to the six-day bike races.

DON: Your Uncle Thurmond sure was a strange man.

MAR: What do you mean—strange?

DON: Well, isn't it odd that a man should pass away and will himself two million dollars?

MAR: I don't think so. Uncle merely figured that if he couldn't take it with him, he'd come back and get it. Don't you believe in returning spirits, John?

DON: No. Anybody that lends me a bottle of bourbon deserves to lose it.

MAR: Don't be funny, John. I'm serious.

DON: Well, I'm sleepy. Put out the light.

MAR: In a minute. You know as well as I do that there's such a thing as reincarnation. Some people come back as cows, or horses, or birds—some people even come back as people.

DON: Mmm.

MAR: What would you like to come back as, John?

DON: I'd like to come back as your Uncle and collect that two million dollars. Blanche, why don't you let me sleep?

MAR: I'm all finished now.

DON: Good.

MAR: John.

DON: Mmm.

MAR: You've had that bed long enough—now let's change places.

DON: What are you talking about? I haven't even closed my eyes yet.

MAR: Well, it's not my fault if you waste your time talking.

DON: I wasn't talking! You were talking!

MAR: Well, nobody asked you to waste your time listening. Come on, John, get up.

DON: (GETTING UP) Get up, get up—I spend half my life getting up. I swear when I get home I'm gonna sleep so long they'll have to inject sleeping pills just to wake me up.

MAR: Oh, go to sleep.

DON: (GETTING INTO COT) Crummy old cot with—Owww!

MAR: What's wrong, John?

DON: What's the idea of piling those calendars in this cot?

MAR: There was no place else to put them. And don't be so fussy, you wouldn't have been able to sleep in that broken cot, anyway.

DON: I can sleep on a barbed-wire fence! Just give me a chance, that's all I ask. For the last time—put out that light!

MAR: All right, don't shout. I'll—John!

DON: What's the matter? What are you staring at me for, Blanche?

MAR: Why have you got that shopping bag hanging from your neck?

DON: It's not a shopping bag.

MAR: Well, I never saw anything like it. What is it?

DON: Oh, you've seen me wear it a hundred times. It's my bourbon bib.

MAR: Bourbon bib!

DON: What are you looking so shocked for? Men wear money belts, don't they?

MAR: I don't see how you can sleep with that thing hanging around your neck.

DON: I can sleep fine. On cold nights I pull the cork out with my teeth and I can drink without taking my hands out from under the covers.

MAR: John Bickerson, sometimes I believe you think more of your bourbon than you do of me...John, I said—

DON: I heard what you said, Blanche. I was just thinking about it.

MAR: What!

DON: I mean—

MAR: I know very well what you mean. Nothing you ever do escapes me...I saw that little byplay at the dinner table tonight.

DON: What are you talking about?

MAR: Never mind.

DON: All right, forget it.

MAR: I saw you flirting with my Aunt Stella.

DON: Oh, now listen, Blanche—

MAR: Don't try to soft-soap me like you did her. I heard every word—I heard you tell her that she looked like my dear departed uncle.

DON:	You didn't hear every word. I told her she looked like your dear departed uncle two days after he departed.
MAR:	I'd like to believe that. I'll bet not a day goes by that you're not making eyes at some woman.
DON:	Oh, cut it out, Blanche. You know I hate women.
MAR:	Well, then you hate me, too.
DON:	You're not a woman, you're my wife! What do you want from me, Blanche!
MAR:	I don't want anything from you, John. I just want you to appreciate the fact that you have a loyal wife.
DON:	I appreciate it.
MAR:	Lots of poor single men don't know what it means to have a wife.
DON:	Poor men.
MAR:	Somebody ought to tell them.
DON:	I'll tell them in the morning.
MAR:	What will you tell them, John?
DON:	I'll tell them a wife is a woman who will stick by you in all the trouble you wouldn't have gotten into if you hadn't married her in the first place. Goodnight, Blanche.
MAR:	Oh, you horrid thing. I'll never speak to you again.
DON:	Just like a woman. When everything else fails you try bribery.
MAR:	Don't talk to me anymore. (CLICK OF SWITCH) Just hush up and go to sleep.
DON:	Go to sleep, she tells me. Drags me three hundred miles to find out she inherited Honest John, and she expects me to sleep. I'll never—sleep—another—(SNORES. PHONE RINGS)
MAR:	John!
DON:	Mmm?
MAR:	The phone—answer it.
DON:	Hello. (PHONE RINGS)
MAR:	Go to the phone and answer it!
DON:	(GETTING OUT OF BED) Who's got the crust to call a man in the middle of—(BUMPS INTO NIGHT TABLE) Owwww! (RECEIVER UP) Hello!

MAN: (FILTER) Hello, John? This is Barney!

DON: Barney! What's the idea of calling me up at two in the morning?

MAN: I didn't know what time it was. I just got back from the Bike races.

DON: What do I care!

MAN: Aaah, stop worrying about your sleep. I need your advice, John. I spent my last cent to come out here and all I got left in the world is ten thousand dollars worth of insurance on my life. What shall I do?

DON: DROP DEAD! (HANGS UP) Never saw it to fail! (GETS INTO BED) First time in my life my wife was ever mad enough not to speak to me, and that bum has to spoil it.

MAR: John.

DON: I thought you weren't talking to me.

MAR: Well, I've changed my mind, John. Other couples patch up their quarrels, why can't we?

DON: We don't have to patch 'em up. We get new ones.

MAR: Don't be like that, John. Just for once can't we go to sleep saying something nice to each other.

DON: Oh, dear.

MAR: I'll start first. Listen, John.

DON: I'm listening.

MAR: John, dear, you're so noble, so generous, so handsome, so much the superior of every man I meet, I just can't help loving you. There. Now what do you see in plain little me to admire?

DON: Well, for one thing you've got good judgement. Goodnight, Blanche.

MAR: Goodnight, John.

(THEME...APPLAUSE)

THE BICKERSONS JUNE 5, 1951 (SHOW #1)

	OPENING
JOHNNY:	CALL…FOR…PHILIP…MORRIS!
MUSIC:	(MUSIC OUT)
VOICE:	BELIEVE…IN…YOURSELF!
HOLBROOK:	Yes, BELIEVE…IN…YOURSELF! *Compare* PHILIP MORRIS, *match* PHILIP MORRIS—*judge* PHILIP MORRIS against *any other brand!* Then…decide for YOURSELF which cigarette is milder…tastier…more enjoyable. BELIEVE IN YOURSELF…and you'll believe in PHILIP MORRIES, America's FINEST CIGARETTE!
JOHNNY:	CALL…FOR…PHILIP…MORRIS!
MUSIC:	(THEME UP TO FINISH)
ANN:	And now, the makers of Philip Morris Cigarettes are pleased to present the first in a new series of programs starring Miss Frances Langford and Mr. Lew Parker. Several seasons ago radio listeners were mildly startled by the introduction of one of the most unconventional married couples in microphone history. I'm referring, of course, to Philip Rapp's humorous creation "The Bickersons." Tonight, for the first time, you will hear them in their own half hour program—an unretouched picture of domestic tranquility. Before they begin, however, I think it only fair that you meet the long-suffering, short-napping John Bickerson, America's Number One somnophiliac, so ably portrayed by America's Number Two somnophiliac—Lew Parker! Mr. Parker.
	(APPLAUSE)
PARK:	Thank you, ladies and gentlemen, and good vening.
ANN:	Mr. Parker, what is a somnophiliac?
PARK:	It's an unforgiveable combination of Latin and Greek roots and it probably means lover of sleep. There's no such word.
ANN:	Well, it'll do until a better one comes along. Nobody loves sleep more than John Bickerson.

PARK: And, certainly, nobody sleeps less. We'll soon give you a practical demonstration of that, but first I want to introduce the young lady who breathes life into that slumber-destroying, but quite understandable female, Blanche Bickersons. It is with great pleasure that we present the gracious person who has earned the undying love and gratitude of our boys both here and overseas for her tireless efforts in still another role, the Purple Heart Girl—Miss Frances Langford!

(APPLAUSE)

LANG: Thank you.

PARK: Frances, before we put the gloves on for our Bickerson stint I have a little favor to ask of you

LANG: Anything you want, Lew.

PARK: It isn't for me, although I'm sure I'll enjoy it. A couple of weeks ago when you were entertaining the servicemen at the Long Beach Veterans Hospital one of the boys fell in love with you.

LANG: Only one?

PARK: Well, this one's doing something about it. He's written a letter asking that you sing a song especially for him. His name is Terry Amico of Ward N-3, and the song he wants is "   ." Okay, Frances?

LANG: Nothing would give me greater pleasure.

SONG: LANG & ORCH.

(APPLAUSE)

COMMERCIAL

ANN: Now, ladies and gentlemen, here are Frances Langford and Lew Parker as John and Blanche Bickerson in "The Honeymoon Is Over"!

THEME: (SOFT AND PLAINTIVE)

ANN: In the Bickerson bedroom there is an infernal machine. With the persistent, inexorable ticking common to all time-bombs it gradually approaches the hour that will shatter the ears and destroy the happiness of the unsuspecting John. It's a matter of seconds now—eight, seven, six, five, four, three, two, one—

SOUND: A LOUD ALARM CLOCK...SUSTAINED RING

PARK: I wish I was dead!...All right, all right, all right!

SOUND: HE THROTTLES THE CLOCK...STRUGGLES OUT OF BED

PARK:	Blanche!…Blanche!
LANG:	(OFF) Wait a minute—I'm putting a ribbon in my hair.
PARK:	Where you going?
LANG:	(ON) I'm not going anywhere. I just thought I'd like to look nice this morning.
PARK:	Why?
LANG:	I knew you'd forget it…You did forget it!…Today happens to be our wedding anniversary.
PARK:	I didn't forget it.
LANG:	Then why didn't you say something?
PARK:	I just opened my eyes!
LANG:	You forgot it.
PARK:	I tell you I didn't forget it, but even if I did you'd remind me of it.
LANG:	Well? We've been married eight years. What do you want to do?
PARK:	Nothing. It's too late to do anything about it.
LANG:	I mean haven't you got any plans for tonight?
PARK:	Sure. I've got it all worked out…I'm gonna take you to dinner and a burlesque show.
LANG:	No, you're not. I'm having a party tonight.
PARK:	Then what did you ask me for?
LANG:	Well, I wanted to surprise you. The whole thing was my sister Clara's idea, and we're just having a few close friends and relatives.
PARK:	Close relatives…Where's my pants? Somebody stole my pants!
LANG:	Nobody stole your pants.
PARK:	I just looked under the bed and they're not there. My shoes are missing from the waste-basket, too.
LANG:	Nothing's missing, John. Your pants are on a hanger in the closet, your shoes are in the shoe-rack.
PARK:	How'd they get there?
LANG:	I put them there.
PARK:	Well, I wish you'd quit throwing my things around like that. By the time I find everything I'll be late for work.
LANG:	You won't be late. Here are your pants.

PARK: Thanks…Blanche! These aren't my pants!

LANG: Then whose pants are they?

PARK: That's a good question…only I should be asking it.

LANG: Don't be so funny in the morning. They were baggy so I pressed them.

PARK: Baggy.

LANG: It took me an hour to find the right crease. Be careful you don't wrinkle them.

PARK: What's the difference? I like my pants to look lived in.

LANG: You're dragging the cuffs on the floor! Hold your trouser legs with your left hand and step in with your right foot.

PARK: Blanche—I've been putting on my own pants for thirty years, I don't need you to foreman the job!…Hand me my tie.

LANG: Which one?

PARK: It doesn't matter. I wanna use it for a belt—my suspenders are broken.

LANG: Why don't you wear your belt?

PARK: I'm using it to keep the soles from falling off my shoes.

LANG: John Bickerson! Your shoes are—

PARK: I know it! I haven't got a belt…What have you done to my pants?

LANG: What's the matter with them?

PARK: The crease belongs in front, not straight down from the side pockets! I'll look like a freak.

LANG: Oh, nobody's going to look at you.

PARK: Nobody's gonna look at me. Give me a sailor cap and I'll join the Navy!

LANG: It wouldn't hurt you. Sailors make good money. Barney's friend, Rudy, joined the Navy and he worked himself up from able-bodied stoker—

PARK: I don't care about Barney's friend! I'm not joining the Navy and I'm not gonna wear these pants!

LANG: Don't wear them. Take them off and put on your old grey suit.

PARK: I haven't got time. Where's my shirt?

LANG: Your coffee's getting cold.

PARK: I don't want any coffee! Where'd you hide my shirt?

LANG: I didn't hide it anywhere.

PARK: Well, where is it?

LANG: I dropped it around the canary's cage.

PARK: Is my shirt the only rag you can find to cover that cage with?

LANG: It hasn't hurt it any, has it?

PARK: No, but I don't like the way that bird pokes into my pockets. Every time I take a cigarette out I'm smoking birdseed. Why do you have to cover the cage, anyway?

LANG: The canary is sensitive to light.

PARK: Well, get him a pair of sunglasses and leave my shirt alone!

LANG: Can't you leave it over the cage till you finish your coffee?

PARK: Nothing doing—no bird's gonna sleep later than I do.

SOUND: RUSTLE OF SHIRT BEING REMOVED...CANARY TRILLS

PARK: Ahhh—shut up!

(THE CANARY STOPS)

LANG: Why must you be so mean on our anniversary?

PARK: Blanche, I'm not mean, I'm worried. I haven't sold a single vacuum cleaner for four weeks.

LANG: You sold one on Thursday.

PARK: I know—but we bought it! I had to sell something to keep from getting fired. I'd like to take it back, Blanche—I can't make the payments on it.

LANG: You leave it alone! We'll need it when we get a carpet Now listen, John, I want you to calm down and drink your coffee. It doesn't matter if you're a few minutes late.

PARK: It does matter. My first call is way on the other side of town, and the woman won't wait.

LANG: You've got to eat some breakfast.

PARK: No time. I've got to shave.

LANG: Then drink your coffee.

PARK: All right, I'll drink my coffee.

LANG: I'll get the toaster.

SOUND: ELECTRIC SHAVER

LANG: If you'd eat a little break—John Bickerson!

(SHAVER STOPS)

PARK: What are you doing, Blanche? Don't pull that plug out!

LANG: I won't have you shaving at the breakfast table!

PARK: There's no plug in the bathroom.

LANG: Then you'll have to use some other kind of razor. Besides, where am I going to plug the toaster?

PARK: Don't plug it. I gotta get out. Where's my hat?

LANG: Aren't you going to finish your coffee?

PARK: Haven't got time.

LANG: Come home early.

PARK: Yeah. I'll see you later, Blanche. Goodbye.

LANG: John!

PARK: What?

LANG: I've been standing here waiting for you to kiss me goodbye and you haven't even looked at me.

PARK: I looked at you.

LANG: What do you mean by that?

PARK: Nothing, Blanche—I'm late.

LANG: Have you got your sample?

PARK: Here it is...This darn vacuum cleaner gets heavier every day. Straighten this hose around my neck, will you, Blanche?

LANG: There...Got everything?

PARK: I guess so...Wait a minute—you got any money?

LANG: There's fifty cents in the sugar bowl.

PARK: Fifty cents!

LANG: You can bring me the change when you come home.

PARKER: Now listen, Blanche—something's gotta be done about this. I can't go down to work like a pauper every day. A man's got to have a couple of dollars in his pocket.

LANG: Well, don't yell at me.

PARKER:	I don't mind going in torn clothes—holes in my socks—but I'm not gonna suffer through those lunches anymore.
LANG:	What's the matter with your lunches?
PARK:	You ought to know—you pack 'em for me. I'm just getting sick of carrying my lunch to work in a paper sack. Whey can't I go to a restaurant like the other fellows—
LANG:	John! What are you talking about? I haven't fixed your lunch for two years!
PARK:	Oh, Blanche! Every morning of my life I find my lunch wrapped in brown paper on the side of the sink!
LANG:	Lunch? That's the garbage!
PARK:	No wonder nobody wants to swap sandwiches with me. Goodbye, Blanche.
LANG:	Goodbye, dear—and happy anniversary.
MUSIC:	BRIDGE
SOUND:	DOOR OPENS & CLOSE
CLARA:	Happy anniversary, Blanche!
LANG:	Oh, thanks, Clara. Where's Barney?
BARNEY:	I'm here…Move away, Clara…What have you done to the place, Blanche?
LANG:	I just fixed it up a little for the party tonight. Did you bring the potato salad, Clara?
CLARA:	Oh, dear. I was going to tell you about that, Blanche. I had a terrible accident with the potato salad.
BARNEY:	I ate it.
LANG:	Oh. Well, we'll get along without it. Don't feel bad about it, Barney.
BARNEY:	Who feels bad?
CLARA:	Keep quiet, Barney. I would have made some more, Blanche, only I ran out of potatoes.
LANG:	That's all right. I've got plenty of stuff. I've been cooking all morning.
BARNEY:	What did you do to your hair?
LANG:	Why, I had it waved. What's wrong with it?
BARNEY:	Nothing.…Clara, it's getting late. Why don't you tell her?

LANG:	Tell me what?
CLARA:	Well, this is going to come as a terrible disappointment to you, Blanche, but Barney can't come to the party tonight.
LANG:	Oh, really?
BARNEY:	What kind of terrible disappointment? She don't care if I come to the party tonight! I don't even care myself…Go on and tell her.
CLARA:	Why don't you tell her?
BARNEY:	All right, I will.
CLARA:	Barney's been invited to a masquerade party at the United Nations Poolhall. You know, his friend's place?
LANG:	No.
BARNEY:	Tell her already.
CLARA:	Well, anyway, he wants to go and it's a sort of a hard times party. Everybody's going dressed as a bum.
LANG:	Well, what are you telling me for?
CLARA:	I thought maybe he could borrow some of John's clothes.
LANG:	Well, that's a nice thing to say!
CLARA:	Now don't get huffy, Blanche. I was just asking. What does John do with his old clothes?
LANG:	He wears them. I'm sorry, Clara, but I don't think John has—
SOUND:	CLOSET DOOR OPENS
CLARA:	Barney! Come away from that closet.
BARNEY:	Why can't I borrow this old grey suit? Them raglan shoulders are way out of style.
LANG:	Oh, I forgot about that suit. John never wears it and it just hangs there. You can have it, Barney.
BARNEY:	Thanks. The boys'll get a kick out of these open-toed pants…You coming, Clara?
CLARA:	In a minute. Blanche, are you sure you don't want me to make some potato salad for you? The party isn't till seven o'clock, and there's plenty of time.
LANG:	Well, if it isn't any trouble—
CLARA:	Of course not. Just lend me a few pounds of potatoes and I'll whip it right up.

LANG:	I haven't got any potatoes.
CLARA:	Well, let's forget about it then. It'll give me a chance to catch up on my housework, you know?
LANG:	Yes.
CLARA:	I wonder if you'd mind lending me your vacuum cleaner, Blanche?
LANG:	I can't do that, Clara. It's never been used, it's still in the box.
CLARA:	Oh. Well, where's John's sample?
LANG:	He's using it for demonstrations! How do you suppose he sells vacuum cleaners?
CLARA:	With his disposition, I'll never know. Let's go, Barney.
MUSIC:	BRIDGE
SOUND:	DOOR CHIMES…DOOR OPENS
PARK:	Good morning, Madam. I'm from the Eagle Appliance, paying a call in answer to your—
WOMAN:	Oh, I'm sorry—you're twenty minutes late and I've got an appointment at the dentist.
PARK:	I'll only take a few minutes of your—
WOMAN:	I can't wait. I'm getting my bridge today.
PARK:	But I just want you to see—
WOMAN:	I'm sorry, not now. I've got to get to my dentist.
SOUND:	DOOR SLAM
PARK:	What good are teeth if your house is dirty?…Oh, well….
SOUND:	FOOTSTEPS FADING OFF…THEN FADE IN AGAIN…WALKS UP PORCH STEPS…DOORBELL….DOOR OPENS
MAN:	Yeah?
PARK:	Good morning, sir. Is your wife in?
MAN:	What's it about?
PARK:	Well, she dropped us a card requesting a demonstration.
MAN:	Of what?
PARK:	We sell vacuum cleaners.
MAN:	Oh, she changed her mind. I bought her a new broom.

SOUND:	DOOR SLAM...FOOTSTEPS GOING DOWN STAIRS..FADE OUT...THEN FADE IN AGAIN WEARILY.
PARK:	(OVER FOOTSTEPS) How do you like that...Five o'clock and I haven't even got a foot in a door yet. (FOOTSTEPS STOP) Well, this is my last call.
SOUND:	DOOR-KNOCKER
PARK:	I'll have to high-pressure this one...I've been giving up too easy.
SOUND:	DOOR OPENS
PARK:	(BRISKLY) Good afternoon, madam, I represent the Eagle Appliance Company and I'm about to give you a demonstration that will simply amaze you.
WOMAN:	I haven't time now.
PARK:	If you'll just follow me into your living room—Ahhh, here we are, and a charming room it is, too. Now then, let's just empty these ashtrays on the floor.
SOUND:	CLINKING OF ASHTRAYS BEING EMPTIED
WOMAN:	What are you doing?
PARK:	How lucky! The waste-basket is full, too! Well, we'll just scatter this junk all over the place.
SOUND:	SCATTERS JUNK ON FLOOR...DROPS WASTEBASKET.
WOMAN:	Listen, you—stop that!
PARK:	Don't be alarmed, Madam...Now I'm going to go over this rug just once—and if this vacuum cleaner doesn't pick up every single last speck of this filth I'll eat it!
WOMAN:	Well, you better start eating, Mister—our electricity's been shut off!
MUSIC:	BRIDGE
SOUND:	TYPEWRITER...PHONE RINGS...TYPING STOPS...RECEIVER UP.
MAN:	Eagle Appliance Company.
LANG:	(FILTER) This is Mrs. Bickerson, may I speak to my husband, please?
MAN:	He hasn't come in off his route yet.
LANG:	He hasn't? But it's seven-thirty.
MAN:	Yeah. He must be having a good day.

LANG:	Oh. Well, we're having an anniversary party tonight and I didn't want him to be late.
MAN:	I'll tell him you called when he comes in, Mrs. Bickerson.
LANG:	Thank you…Goodbye.
MAN:	Goodbye.
SOUND:	RECEIVER DOWN…TYPING…DOOR OPENS AND CLOSES…TYPING STOPS
MAN:	Hy'a, Bickerson…Your wife just called.
PARK:	Yeah.
SOUND:	HEAVY OBJECT DROPPED TO FLOOR
MAN:	Hey, watch it. You'll bust that vacuum cleaner dropping it that way.
PARK:	What do I care! Look what it's done to me—one of my arms is a foot longer than the other. My feet are killing me, too.
MAN:	She's worried about you being late for the party.
PARK:	Yeah. Hand me those sneakers, will you?
MAN:	Here. Sneakers are bad for your feet.
PARK:	They're my feet.
MAN:	You don't seem too happy. How'd it go today?
PARK:	The only nibble I had all day was from a dog.
MAN:	Well, tomorrow's another day.
PARK:	I'm glad you thought of that, Marvin.
MAN:	It's your anniversary, huh?
PARK:	Yeah.
MAN:	What's the matter, forget to get her a present?
PARK:	I think I got her one present too many. I picked up a couple of cheap things at first—then I got sentimental and bought her a diamond ring.
MAN:	A diamond ring!
PARK:	On time. Nothing down and ten dollars a week for life! I'm three weeks behind on the first payment…Listen, Marvin—
MAN:	Oh, no! No, you don't, Bickerson! I've got no money, and if I did have any I wouldn't lend it to you—you still owe me four dollars.
JOHN:	I know, but—

MAN:	Nothing doing. If you need money, sell a vacuum cleaner.
JOHN:	Hmm?...Yeah...Sell a vacuum cleaner...Yeah....
MUSIC:	BRIDGE
SOUND:	STORE BELL TINKLES AS DOOR OPENS...THUD OF HEAVY OBJECT BEING DROPPED ON COUNTER
JOHN:	How much will you give me on this vacuum cleaner?
MAN:	Does it work?
JOHN:	It's brand new—right off the shelf...How much?
MAN:	From the Eagle Appliance Company, huh? Well, I'll call them up and see what it lists for.
JOHN:	Look I'm in a hurry...It's worth a hundred and fifteen bucks. Give me twenty and let me get out of here.
MAN:	Well, all right...you wait here, I'll go make out the ticket
JOHN:	Don't be long, will you?
MAN:	Be right back.
SOUND:	DOOR OPENS AND CLOSES...DIALING OF PHONE
COP:	(FILTER) Police Headquarters.
MAN:	This is the Argyle Pawn Shop. I think I've got the man you've been looking for, the cat burglar.
COP:	What's your address, please?
MAN:	I'm on the corner of Sixth and Elm. He just came in and tried to sell me a brand new vacuum cleaner.
COP:	Does the suspect answer the description in the circular?
MAN:	Well, he's about five-foot ten...Around a hundred and eighty pounds...
COP:	Hair and eyes?
MAN:	Black and blue.
COP:	Mm-hmm. Did you happen to notice whether he was wearing sneakers?
MAN:	By George! I believe he is!
COP:	We'll send a squad car right over. Try to stall him till we get there.
MUSIC:	BRIDGE
SOUND:	BABBLE OF VOICES...PEOPLE SAYING GOODNIGHT...VOICES FADE

DOC:		It was a wonderful anniversary party, Mrs. Bickerson. Too bad John couldn't make it.
LANG:		I can't understand it, Doctor Hersey. He's never been this late before.
DOC:		Well, I wouldn't worry about it. He probably got tied up with some tough customer.
LANG:		Probably.
DOC:		Well, good night, and thanks again.
LANG:		Goodnight, Doctor.
SOUND:		DOOR SLAM…FOOTSTEPS GOING DOWNSTAIRS…STREET DOOR OPENS…SIREN FADE IN…CAR PULLS UP TO CURB…CAR DOOR OPENS AND CLOSES.
PARK:		Thanks, Officer…I'll be over in the morning to claim the vacuum cleaner. And please make sure they take my name off the blotter.
SOUND:		CAR PULLS AWAY
DOC:		(OVER SOUND) Bickerson! What happened?
PARK:		Oh, hello, Doc. Nothing—it's a long story. I'll tell you about it some other time.
DOC:		Oh. Well, I certainly enjoyed your anniversary. Too bad you couldn't be with us—but there'll always be another anniversary.
PARK:		Yeah. Too bad.
DOC:		Say, you better get some rest, old man. You look done in.
PARK:		I do, huh?
DOC:		Well, goodnight. And happy anniversary.
PARK:		Thanks.
DOC:		Oh—er—I didn't want to tell your wife, Bickerson—but I left a little something for you on the hall table.
PARK:		Well, thanks.
DOC:		You needn't pay it until the tenth. You can mail it in with last month's bill.
PARK:		Thanks.
DOC:		Don't mention it. Now you run along and get some sleep. And if you have a little time I'd advise you to come to my office for a checkup. I'd like fluroscoping you. (AS HE WALKS AWAY…CALLS) Don't forget now! Drop in!

PARK: Drop dead! He'd like to fluoroscope me...He's been fluroscoping me for years...Oh, I'm dead on my feet—and I'll probably be up all night answering Blanche's questions...What a life!.....If I tell her the truth she won't talk to me for a week. (SLIGHT PAUSE) So I'll tell her the truth!

MUSIC: PLAYOFF

RECORDING

BOB: Hello there, this is Bob Pfeiffer. While we've been arranging our microphone here in the lobby of the Battle House in Mobile, Alabama, my assistant has been locating a volunteer to try the Philip Morris nose test. Frank, how are you doing?

FRANK: OK, Bob. Bob, I'd like you to meet Mr. Richard Hewitt, from Fairhope, Alabama. Mr. Hewitt is not a Philip Morris smoker.

BOB: Thanks, Frank. Mr. Hewitt, it's mighty nice meeting you.

HEWITT: Very glad to meet you, Bob.

BOB: Now about the test. Would you do me one favor? For obvious reasons, we don't want you to refer to your present cigarette by its brand name. Is that OK?

HEWITT: That's OK.

BOB: Now I'd like to give you a Philip Morris cigarette, Mr. Hewitt. I wonder if you have one of your own brand handy, do you?

HEWITT: Right here.

BOB: Fine. Now I want you to light up one of these two cigarettes. It doesn't matter which one you try first. So you make the choice.

HEWITT: All right.

BOB: Which one do you want to try first, sir?

HEWITT: My own brand.

BOB: Your own brand first. I see it's also one of the leading brands. Now I'll give you a light, then I want you to take a puff, don't inhale, and slowly let the smoke come through your nose. All right, sir. That was your own brand first. Is that correct?

HEWITT: That's right.

BOB: All right. Let's try exactly the same test now with the Philip Morris. Remember, I'll give you a light, then take a puff, don't inhale, and slowly let the smoke come through your nose. All right, Mr. Hewitt. You tried the test by your choice, first with your own brand, then with the Philip Morris, and you made exactly the same

	test with both. Now what we want are your reactions. Did you notice any difference between the two cigarettes?
HEWITT:	Oh, I think there's a little less, or quite a bit less, burn in the Philip Morris.
BOB:	Thank you very much, Mr. Hewitt.
	END OF RECORDING
THEME:	(SOFT AND PLAINTIVE)
ANN:	The Bickersons have retired. Blanche Bickerson lies tense and sleepless in the dark as poor husband John, tortured by the guilt of having missed his own anniversary party, suffers another attack of intermittent insomnia, or Woodchopper's Syndrome…Listen.
PARK:	(SNORES LUSTILY…WHINES…SNORES AND WHIHES…ABROKEN RHYTHM SNORE FOLLOWED BY A WHINE)
LANG:	He sounds like he swallowed The Thing!
PARK:	(SNORES AND GIGGLES)
LANG:	Oh dear.
PARK:	(SNORES AND GIGGLES AGAIN)
LANG:	John.
PARK:	Mmm.
LANG:	Turn over on your side. Go on!
PARK:	(A PROTESTING WHINE) Mmmmmmm.
LANG:	Stop it, stop it, stop it!
PARK:	Stop it, Blanche. Wassamatter? Wassamatter, Blanche?
LANG:	That whining and giggling and grunting and snarling! It's driving me crazy!
PARK:	Me too, Blanche. Who's doing it?
LANG:	You're doing it! It amazes me that you can sleep at all with your guilty conscience.
PARK:	Not guilty. Put out the lights.
LANG:	I will not! I've got plenty to say to you.
PARK:	Oh dear.
LANG:	You don't like to listen because you can't stand to hear the truth.

PARK: Blanche, what's the matter with you? It's three o'clock in the morning! You had a good time tonight, now why don't you let me sleep?

LANG: I had a miserable time. It was the unhappiest anniversary I ever spent. Why didn't you show up for the party, John?

PARK: I told you. I got stuck at the office.

LANG: I'd like to believe that.

PARK: Blanche, I've had a rough day. I went to work at seven this morning—no lunch, no dinner—and now I'd like to get a little rest.

LANG: I suppose you think I loafed all day?

PARK: Mmmm.

LANG: I worked my fingers to the bone getting ready for the party and never had one minute's enjoyment. I just got through washing the dishes and sweeping the floor, but I still haven't gotten rid of the crumbs in the kitchen.

PARK: I thought they all went home.

LANG: That isn't a bit funny, John Bickerson. Everybody who came tonight was sweet and thoughtful and they all brought presents.

PARK: Good.

LANG: That's more than you did. The Homers were here and they brought something—the Hydes were here and they brought something—even my sister Clara was here.

PARK: What did *she* take?

LANG: She didn't take anything. And if she didn't bring a present it's because she can't afford it. Barney isn't working.

PARK: He never works.

LANG: He does, too. It's just that he's recovering from his accident.

PARK: What accident?

LANG: When he was out looking for a job last month he tripped over a barrel and two cases of bourbon fell on his head.

PARK: Well, it's the first time the drinks were ever on him. Go to sleep, Blanche.

LANG: That's the kind of talk I get on my wedding anniversary. No hug, no kiss, no affection. Just go to sleep.

PARK: Okay—goodnight.

LANG: You said you didn't have dinner—why didn't you eat something when you came home?

PARK: There wasn't anything.

LANG: Well, who told you to come home so late? Clara took what was left of the ham and Doctor Hersey cleaned up the spaghetti. I gave Nature Boy the rest of the chicken.

PARK: Who's Nature Boy?

LANG: Our cat. Did I hear him yell when you came in?

PARK: I stepped on him.

LANG: What did you do that for?

PARK: I was fighting him for the chicken bones! What do you mean what did I do that for? It was dark and he got under my feet!

LANG: You never liked that cat.

PARK: I like him fine.

LANG: The first night I brought him home you gave him a nasty look.

PARK: He's got a nasty look, all right - but I didn't give it to him. Just keep him out of my way.

LANG: You hated the other cat we had.

PARK: Which other cat?

LANG: Shiners. The big black one.

PARK: Shiners?

LANG: You know—the one you said committed suicide after you caught him drinking your bourbon.

PARK: He did commit suicide.

LANG: I'd love to believe that.

PARK: What are you hinting at, Blanche? Cats have been known to commit suicide.

LANG: They don't hang themselves.

PARK: He didn't hang himself! He got his neck tangled in a ball of twine and I was trying to loosen it when you walked in. Don't start making me into a cat killer!

LANG: A man who would forget his own anniversary is capable of anything.

PARK: I tell you I didn't forget.

LANG: Not even an anniversary card. The least you could have done was send me a card.

PARK: I did send you a card. I told you fifty times I sent you a card. It must have got lost in the mail.

LANG: Then why didn't you send another one?

PARK: How did I know it was gonna get lost?

LANG: It's a funny thing but everybody else's card got here.

PARK: Maybe it'll come tomorrow.

LANG: It'll never come because you didn't send it.

PARK: I tell you I did send it!

LANG: Swear you sent me a card!

PARK: I swear! It was trimmed with lace and it had a wonderful poem on it. I picked it especially for you.

LANG: What did it say on it?

PARK: Go to sleep.

LANG: If you picked it especially for me I want to know what it said.

PARK: It said "Happy Anniversary to my Love—

LANG: That could be anybody.

PARK: Let me finish! It said "Happy Anniversary to My Love—my wife, my life, my turtle dove—life with you is great it seems—I love you more than pork and beans!"

LANG: You're only adding insult to injury.

PARK: Well, how do I know what it said? I can't remember the stupid poetry they put on those things. Put out the lights.

LANG: You torture me every year on our anniversary.

PARK: Oh, dear.

LANG: Am I so old and homely that you can't show any affection or sentiment? Can't you ever find it in your heart to pay me a compliment?

PARK: It won't do any good. All you wanna do is fight! Night and day fight, fight, fight!

LANG: I do not! We'd get along fine if you'd be a little nicer to me. The trouble with you is you're tired of me.

PARK: No—I'm just tired. Goodnight.

LANG:	Look at George Wood. There's a wonderful husband for you. He's been in love with the same woman since the day he was married.
PARK:	Does his wife know about her?
LANG:	Never mind the sarcasm. If you didn't have those evil thoughts you'd make a better husband. I'm not a demanding wife.
PARK:	Mmm.
LANG:	All I ever ask from you is a pleasant smile or a kind word…Wake up, John.
PARK:	What do you want?
LANG:	Say something nice to me!
PARK:	I love you! I adore you! I can't live without you! Now shut up and go to sleep!
LANG:	That's right—scream at me on our wedding anniversary.
PARK:	If you'll just keep quiet for a while I won't scream.
LANG:	I'm going to talk whether you like it or not.
PARK:	I don't like it.
LANG:	Don't forget Mr. Bickerson, I gave you the best years of my life.
PARK:	Were those the best?
LANG:	Keep it up, John. Night after night I go to sleep crying into my pillow. It's soaked through from my tears—and one kiss would make it all perfect.
PARK:	Well, throw over your pillow and I'll kiss it.
LANG:	You see—you're starting again. Is it asking too much of you to be nice to me once a year?
PARK:	I'm always nice to you.
LANG:	You never are! You're perfectly horrid. We'd never have a single argument if you'd just give me a little attention.
PARK:	Nobody gives you as little attention as I do!
LANG:	I'm surprised you admit it. You never take me anywhere—you never show me any courtesy. Do you ever help me on with my coat? Do you ever open a door for me?
PARK:	I'll be glad to open one right now.
LANG:	Last night you took me to the movies and I was never so humiliated in all my life. Such a display of bad manners.

PARK: What bad manners?

LANG: There was one empty seat and I had to race you for it.

PARK: I was running there to hold it for you—some other guy was trying to get it. And my manners are as good as yours. Don't I offer you half the newspaper every morning at breakfast?

LANG: You shouldn't read at the table at all. And when you drive the car up in front of the house you might be a gentleman and help me in.

PARK: Help you in?

LANG: Oh, no. I have to fling the door open and throw myself into the seat.

PARK: Well, I slow down, don't I?

LANG: I'd like to see you act that way with Gloria Gooseby!

PARK: Now don't start with Gloria Gosseby!

LANG: You'd sure be a gentleman if you had her in your car!

PARK: I've had her in my car plenty of times and I've never been a gentleman! I mean, I hate Gloria Gooseby and I wouldn't let her ride on my running board. Why don't you let me sleep, Blanche?

LANG: We've had eight anniversaries and this is the most miserable one of all.

PARK: It's no worse than last year.

LANG: Our whole marriage started on the wrong foot. It was your idea to elope—not mine.

PARK: Yep.

LANG: I wanted to have a real ceremony like all my friends—but you said it was more romantic to elope! We had to be married by a Justice of the Peace.

PARK: Should been the Secretary of War.

LANG: You didn't talk that way then. Why didn't you let me have a big ceremony, John?

PARK: I wasn't working at the time—I didn't have any money.

LANG: Well, you're working now and I want a real wedding…with a big ceremony!

PARK: Okay—I'll arrange it next week.

LANG: You say it but you won't do it. Do it now.

PARK: What?

LANG: Go on—get up and let's get married!

PARK: Are you out of your mind, Blanche? It's almost four o'clock in the morning and I have to go to work at seven. Why do you do this to me? Haven't I suffered enough for one day?

LANG: You haven't suffered half as much as I have. I go to all the trouble of making an anniversary party and you deliberately stay away.

PARK: It wasn't deliberate.

LANG: Why don't you say you're sorry you married me?

PARK: Because I'm not sorry.

LANG: Not at all?

PARK: Not at all.

LANG: Do you hate me?

PARK: You know I do.

LANG: What!

PARK: I mean I don't hate you. Will you please let me sleep?

LANG: I will as soon as you show me the anniversary present you got for me.

PARK: Put out the lights.

LANG: Where is it, John?

PARK: Mmm?

LANG: Where's my anniversary present?

PARK: Oh, you won't like it.

LANG: I know I won't, but I'd like to see it. I hope you didn't spend a lot of money.

PARK: I didn't spend a lot of money.

LANG: Why not?

PARK: Because I didn't have a lot of money. It's just a little old beach bathrobe. It cost eight dollars.

LANG: Eight dollars! Our eighth anniversary and that's all I'm worth to you—eight dollars!

PARK: Now listen, Blanche—

LANG: A dollar a year for washing your shirts, cooking your meals, darning your socks, raising your children—

PARK: We haven't got any children!

LANG: Well, what do you want for a dollar a year?

PARK: Blanche, all I want is sleep. I'll get you something nice tomorrow.

LANG: You told me that yesterday. Today's my anniversary, why couldn't you get me something nice today?

PARK: I did, Blanche. I did get you something—but I can't give it to you now. Go to sleep.

LANG: What did you get me?

PARK: A diamond ring.

LANG: Wake up, John—I'm still talking to you!

PARK: I'm not sleeping, I really bought it for you.

LANG: A diamond ring?

PARK: Yeah.

LANG: Where is it?

PARK: What's the difference? I can't afford it. I'm taking it back in the morning.

LANG: I don't believe it.

PARK: Don't believe it. Put out the lights.

LANG: Show it to me.

PARK: Oh, Blanche, what's the use of looking at it? You can't keep it.

LANG: I just want to see it.

PARK: It's right there in the closet—in the pocket of my old gray suit.

LANG: Your gray suit? You mean the one I gave to Barney?

PARK: That's right. In the left hand pocket of—THE ONE YOU GAVE TO BARNEY! Blanche! You didn't.

LANG: Well, he wanted to dress as a bum and I—

PARK: Blanche! What have you done! That thief will never bring it back and I'll have to—

LANG: Don't get hysterical! I emptied out all the pockets—the stuff's on the dresser. There wasn't any ring box.

PARK: It wasn't in a box—I tied it in my handkerchief...Thank heaven! Here it is. Oh, thank heaven.

LANG: Oh, John! It's beautiful.

PARK: It's gotta go back. Take it off.

LANG: Such a lovely diamond.

PARK: Take it off, Blanche.

LANG: Look at it.

PARK: I've seen it. Take it off.

LANG: Here. Well, it's nice to know you were thinking of me, anyway.

PARK: I'm sorry, Blanche—I did want you to have it—but you can see how impossible—

LANG: I know, dear. You've got enough debts now. It was a wonderful, foolish gesture and I love you for it.

PARK: Keep the ring, Blanche.

LANG: Don't be silly, John—you can't afford—

PARK: Keep it. I'll find a way to pay for it. I'll get an extra job or something. Don't worry. Go to sleep.

LANG: John.

PARK: Mmm.

LANG: You can be so sweet when you want to.

PARK: Mmm.

LANG: I'm so happy. This feels just like when we were first married. You were so kind and considerate. You do love me, don't you, John?

PARK: Yes, Blanche, I love you. Goodnight.

LANG: I remember on our first anniversary you were upset about something and I kissed you goodnight and tucked you in bed like a baby. In the morning everything was fine.

PARK: Go to sleep, Blanche.

LANG: John, would you mind if I just tucked you in bed tonight?

PARK: Okay. Tuck me in.

LANG: Lift your head, dear, so I can straighten the pillow….Now let me get these covers under…Stretch your feet out…There…All tucked in.

PARK: Thanks, darling.

LANG: Are you comfortable, sweetheart?

PARK: Perfectly.

LANG: Are you sure?

PARK: Never felt more comfortable in my life.

LANG: Fine. Now you get up and tuck me in.

PARK:	Goodnight, Blanche.
LANG:	Happy anniversary, John.
MUSIC:	THEME
	APPLAUSE
	CLOSING
MUSIC:	"ON THE TRAIL" THEME
JOHNNY:	CALL...FOR...PHILIP...MORRIS.
HOLBROOK:	Friends, buy a pack of PHILIP MORRIS and try the nose test yourself. Remember...NO CIGARETTE HANGOVER means MORE SMOKING PLEASURE—so...
JOHNNY:	CALL...FOR...PHILLIP...MORRIS!
HOLBROOK:	Be sure to listen next Tuesday night when PHILIP MORRIS again will present The Bickersons. And don't miss the PHILIP MORRIS Playhouse this coming Thursday night over this same station when PHILIP MORRIS will present " ." That's Thursday night for the PHILIP MORRIS Playhouse, over CBS. In the meantime, don't forget to...
JOHNNY:	CALL...FOR...PHILIP...MORRIS!
MUSIC:	OUT
	(APPLAUSE)
HOLBROOK:	The Bickersons came to you, transcribed, from Hollywood, California. John Holbrook speaking.
	THIS IS CBS...THE COLUMBIA BROADCASTING SYSTEM.

THE BICKERSONS SHOW #5 (1951)

PRODUCER: PHIL RAPP
PRODUCT: PHILLIP MORRIS
AGENCY: BIOW
BROADCAST: JULY 10, 1951

ANNCR: Now here are Frances Langford and Lew Parker as radio's most unconventional married couple in Philip Rapp's humorous creation—THE BICKERSONS!

(APPLAUSE)

MUSIC: SOFT AND PLAINTIVE

HOLBROOK: It's seven o'clock in the morning and already the Bickersons are engrossed in conversation. Blanche is in the kitchen chatting with the cat, while John is in the bedroom muttering to himself.

PARK: I never saw it to fail when I'm in a hurry...Blanche...Blanche!

LANG: I can hear you—don't yell.

PARK: I'm late, and there's a button missing off my shirt.

LANG: It isn't missing—it's in the top drawer with your socks. (OPENS DRAWER) Here it is.

PARK: Well, what do you want me to do—paste it on? Why didn't you sew it on my shirt?

LANG: Because I ran out of black thread. Why can't you wear white shirts like everybody else?

PARK: I can't afford the laundry bills. Where's my hat?

LANG: What's the rush this morning?

PARK: I have to go to the airport to meet a very important man. He's an out of town buyer. Maybe I'll invite him here for dinner.

LANG: Don't you dare. I'm ashamed to have anybody see this place.

PARK: What's the matter with this place?

LANG: It's a goat's nest. Listen, John—I want a new apartment.

PARK: I can't let you have a new apartment this year.

LANG: That's what you said last year.

PARK: Well, I kept my word, didn't I? Besides, what's wrong with this apartment?

LANG: Everything. And besides that, it's too small.

PARK: This place is big enough for me. It's got a nice living room, nice dining room, and a nice bedroom.

LANG: Yes, but it's all the same room. I want to move, John.

PARK: We can't afford to move and you know it.

LANG: Well, something's got to be done. The wallpaper's peeling, the plumbing leaks, and I've been asking you for weeks to take care of that big piece of plaster that's missing from the middle of the ceiling!

PARK: I did take care of it! It's all covered.

LANG: I know—but that's no place to hand my mother's picture!

PARK: Well, it was cluttering up the bathroom...I gotta go, Blanche.

LANG: I'm sick of this place. Did you ever look out of the kitchen window?

PARK: Certainly. You can see for miles out of it.

LANG: Miles? You know very well the kitchen window opens on an airshaft.

PARK: Well, you can look straight up, can't you?...Blanche, it's late.

LANG: How do you expect me to invite my friends to this dungeon?

PARK: Don't invite them.

LANG: I have to. Tomorrow's the meeting of the Ladies Assistance League and it's my turn to give the luncheon.

PARK: Why do you have to give it?

LANG: Because I'm head of one of the committees. We do charity work For the Young, Old and Helpless. I'm the Helpless Chairman.

PARK: I might have known it.

LANG: They'll take one look at this place and put us on their charity list. We've got to get a new apartment.

PARK: Blanche, you're making a mountain out of a molehill! Lots of people would give their eye-teeth to have this lovely place. Besides, we've still got nine months to go on our lease.

LANG: We could sublet it.

PARK:	Who'd want to sublet this goat's nest?
LANG:	It's not as bad as you think. It's close to transportation and the building has an elevator.
PARK:	What good is that? We live on the ground floor.
LANG:	I know I could sublet it if you'd only let me try.
PARK:	You're wasting your time, Blanche…Nobody but a complete idiot would rent this crumb joint.
LANG:	You rented it the day you married me!
PARK:	Well that proves it…Goodbye, Blanche.
SOUND:	DOOR SLAM
MUSIC:	BRIDGE
MAN:	Yes, madam—can I help you?
LANG:	I'd like to place a classified ad to sublet my apartment.
MAN:	All right…Name and address, please?
LANG:	Mrs. John Bickerson, 322 West Clump Street.
MAN:	Nice neighborhood…Now if you'll describe your apartment, Mrs. Bickerson, I'll help you frame the ad.
LANG:	Well, it's a lovely apartment—so light and cheery—sunlight streaming in all day—I just hate to give it up.
MAN:	How many rooms?
LANG:	Well, we have an enormous bedroom and the living room and dining room are just the same. My husband and I have been living there for eight years and it's been like one long honeymoon.
MAN:	Is there a large kitchen?
LANG:	The kitchen is the nicest room in the apartment. And it has such an exciting view—I just love to watch the birds from my kitchen window. I think that's everything…Oh, yes! The whole place is done in antique wallpaper, and the building has an elevator.
MAN:	That ought to do it…How does this sound, Mrs. Bickerson? "Lovely, large, sunny honeymoon haven in exclusive neighborhood. Beautiful view. Master bedroom adjoins tastefully decorated living and dining rooms. All modern facilities including elevator. Apartment scaled for luxurious living." What is the rent Mrs. Bickerson?
LANG:	Forty dollars a month.
MAN:	Forty dollars a month?

LANG: That's right...Will that appear in tomorrow's paper?

MAN: No.

LANG: Why not?

MAN: It sounds so attractive, I'll rent it myself!

MUSIC: BRIDGE

MAN: (LOUDSPEAKER) Flight Nine for Chicago, and New York now leaving from Gate Seven.

SOUND: RUNNING FOOTSTEPS FADE IN

PARK: Excuse me...How long ago did Flight Thirteen get in?

MAN: Flight Thirteen?...Arrived on time at eight-oh-five...That's an hour and a half ago.

PARK: Oh. I was supposed to meet somebody on that flight, I hope he's still here. Look, have you seen a kind of tall, cadaverous-looking man, with a big nose, and sort of red-rimmed, little, pig-like eyes?

MAN: (CONFIDENTIALLY) Yes, I have.

PARK: Good. Where is he?

MAN: (SOTTO) He's standing right behind you.

RACKER: Hello, Bickerson.

PARK: Oh...Hello, Mr. Racker. I'm sorry I—

RACKER: Get my bags.

PARK: Yes sir...I certainly appreciate this opportunity to pick you up. Before we go, would you care to have a look at the airport?

RACKER: I've been looking at it for two hours.

PARK: I'm sorry I was late. I had a little—

RACKER: Where's your car?

PARK: That's why I'm late—I ran out of gas. But now that I'm here I'll take care of everything, you can depend on that. So you just—

RACKER: Get a cab.

PARK: Yes, sir. Have one in a minute. Soon as I gather these bags. It's a lovely trip out here by place, isn't it?

RACKER: Didn't sleep a wink.

PARK: You didn't.

RACKER: No. That's how my little pig eyes got so red-rimmed!

PARK: Oh...Well, I've got all your bags. Follow me, sir, and I'll get a cab.

SOUND: FOOTSTEPS

PARK: (OVER SOUND) Yes sir, I don't mind telling you you've got a surprise in store for you—just wait till you see our new line of bowling balls. If I say so myself, they're completely different.

RACKER: What are they—square?

PARK: That's very amusing, sir. But the finger grip has been completely retooled. Yes sir, for 1951 the two-holer is out!...And we've got the sweetest little eighteen-ounce three-holer you've ever seen. I just happen to have one with me, and—

RACKER: Bickerson, I'm in no mood to discuss Bowling balls!...Where am I staying?

PARK: Where?

RACKER: What hotel?

PARK: Hotel?

RACKER: You got my wire to make a reservation for me, didn't you?

PARK: Wire?

SOUND: FOOTSTEPS STOP ABRUPTLY

RACKER: You mean you didn't get me a reservation?

PARK: Well I—

RACKER: There's a convention in town. Everything will be booked solid.

PARK: Well sir, I was hoping—that is, my wife and I would be honored if you'd say with us.

RACKER: With you?

PARK: We've been sort of looking forward to your visit and—well, it isn't often we get a chance to entertain, but—

RACKER: Well...I wouldn't want to inconvenience you...

PARK: Oh, it's no trouble—we'll just put up a cot in the kitchen.

RACKER: Put down my bags.

PARK: I'm sure you'll be very comfortable—

RACKER: Give me those bags.

PARK: Where are you going, Mr. Racker?

RACKER: I'm taking the next plane to Seattle.

PARK: Aren't you even going to look at my bowling balls?

RACKER: I'm buying them in Seattle.

PARK: If you'll just feel the grip on this ball, I know you'll change your mind about leaving.

RACKER: Bickerson, don't make me miss this plane.

PARK: It's the smoothest job on the market—no rough edges—notice how my fingers slip out of the holes— Oops!

SOUND: BOWLING BALL DROPPING

RACKER: Owwww!

PARK: Well— have a nice trip, Mr. Racker.

MUSIC: BRIDGE

SOUND: TYPEWRITER...PHONE RINGS...TYPEWRITER STOPS...RECEIVER UP

PARK: Acme Bowling Alley Equipment Company. Bickerson speaking.

LANG: (FILTER) John, this is Blanche. I've got the most wonderful news. I just rented a new apartment.

PARK: That's fine, I've just been demoted to office boy.

LANG: Wait till you see it! It's got an extra bedroom, all the doors have doorknobs, and—

PARK: What did you do that for? I told you we couldn't afford it. How am I going to pay for two places at once?

LANG: You don't have to. I sublet ours before I rented this new one.

PARK: I can't believe it.

LANG: Well, it's true. The man is coming over to sign the lease tonight. And you better be home at six o'clock.

PARK: I can't, Blanche, I've got to pick up my car.

LANG: What happened to your car?

PARK: I ran out of gas! I wish you'd stop using my gasoline for cleaning fluid!

LANG: I only used a little, and your gas tank was almost empty anyway.

PARK: It was not, I put in a fifth yesterday!

LANG: Well, you can pick your car up tomorrow. Take the bus home. There is a lot of fixing to do before we show this apartment.

PARK:	All right, all right.
LANG:	And John—
PARK:	What?
LANG:	Is there anyone else in the office right now?
PARK:	No, why?
LANG:	Steal a half-dozen erasers, the wallpaper is in horrible shape.
MUSIC:	BRIDGE
SOUND:	BUS MOTOR IDLING…RING OF COINS IN SLOT
SOUND:	BUS STARTS…
PARK:	Hold it driver!…(LEAPS ABOARD)…Almost broke my leg!…Excuse me…Could you move over, mister?
MAN:	I wonder if you'd sit by the window, I have to get off in a few blocks.
PARK:	I think I do, too—but I'm not sure. I don't usually come home this way.
MAN:	I understand. I have a few once in awhile myself.
PARK:	No, I mean by bus. I generally drive, but my car broke down. Would have to happen on the day I'm moving.
MAN:	That's a coincidence. I'm moving, too.
PARK:	Really?
MAN:	Funny how I got this apartment. I've been working in the Classified Ads Section of the *Times* for seven years and never came across anything decent. But today I landed one for me and my family that's just a dream.
PARK:	You ought to see the nightmare we're getting out of.
MAN:	I've got a nice apartment now, but it's too small for my wife and four kids.
PARK:	We had the same problem. Our pigsty was too crowded for just me and my wife. Imagine spending eight years in a one-room apartment with no exposure and early American plumbing!
MAN:	Sounds awful.
PARK:	The whole place is falling apart. Take the bathroom. Every morning when I open the cabinet to get my toothpaste—the whole medicine chest comes right off the wall!
MAN:	(LAUGHING) No!

PARK:	Yeah—and I have such arguments with the man next door through the hole. Serves him right, though—he keeps me up all night with his snoring.
MAN:	How did you manage to unload a joint like that?
PARK:	I'm subletting it to some sucker.
MAN:	Won't he get wise when he sees it?
PARK:	Not after I get through with it. When he comes in to sign the lease, the windows will be shut, incense will be burning. And he'll never know how close we are to the garbage incinerator.
MAN:	Say, that's pretty tricky.
PARK:	That's nothing. The minute I get home I'm gonna nail some branches outside the kitchen window.
MAN:	What for?
PARK:	He'll think he's looking at a park instead of an airshaft. (BUS COMES TO STOP) And after I plug the leaky faucets with corks—
MAN:	Excuse me for interrupting, but this is where I get off.
PARK:	Oh…Hey—wait a minute. I get off here, too.
SOUND:	FOOTSTEPS OFF BUS…BUS PULLS AWAY.
PARK:	Well, so long.
MAN:	So long.
SOUND:	FOOTSTEPS
MAN:	Oh…Going my way?
PARK:	No—I'm going in this building right here.
SOUND:	DOOR OPENS
PARK:	You, too?
MAN:	Uh-huh…The apartment I'm going to rent is in this building.
PARK:	Really.
MAN:	Yes…You visiting someone here?
PARK:	No, I live here. Say, before you go to your new apartment why don't you come look at mine? I want you to have a few laughs.
SOUND:	KEY IN LOCK
MAN:	Thanks, but I haven't got time…Where's apartment 1C?
SOUND:	DOOR OPENS

PARK:	This is it. I— (A DEAD VOICE) Did you say 1C?
MAN:	(IN THE SAME TONE) Did you say this is it?
PARK:	Listen—I hope you didn't take me seriously with my little jokes about the apartment.
LANG:	(OFF) Is that you, John?
PARK:	Just a minute.
LANG:	(CALLS) Well, hurry up and give me a hand before the new tenant gets here. The bathtub slid out into the kitchen again!
MUSIC:	PLAYOFF
	INSERT COMMERCIAL
ANNCR:	Now back to Frances Langford and Lew Parker as John and Blanche Bickerson in "The Honeymoon Is Over."
THEME:	(SOFT AND PLAINTIVE)
ANNCR:	Well, it takes a man of courage to admit that he's acted like a fool and made a costly mistake—so naturally John Bickerson hasn't yet told his wife what became of her prospective tenant. But a little thing like having an extra apartment couldn't prevent Blanche from realizing her fondest dream—a new and larger home. It is just past midnight and the moving man is carting the last of the Bickerson belongings into the spacious three-room apartment (SOUND OF THINGS BEING UNLOADED) as the watchful Blanche supervises the unloading…Listen.
LANG:	No—wait! Put that in the bedroom…The bureau goes into the other room to the left.
MAN:	Yes, ma'am.
LANG:	I never realized we had so much stuff. I just can't bear to throw anything away.
MAN:	No, ma'am.
LANG:	I guess all married people are like that. Are you married?
MAN:	No. ma'am. I walk this way from carrying heavy furniture.
LANG:	Oh. Have you got all the large pieces in?
MAN:	Yes, ma'am. Where do you want this mummy?
LANG:	Mummy! That's my husband! Put him down! John!…John!
PARK:	(SLEEPY) Mmmm. Wassamatter, Blanche?
LANG:	I swear I never saw a man like you! You can't be that sleepy!

PARK: Very sleepy.

MAN: I got one more barrel to bring in.

PARK: Bring it.

SOUND: FOOTSTEPS RECEDING

LANG: You ought to be ashamed of yourself. You might at least offer to help that poor little moving man.

PARK: I did help him.

LANG: You did not.

PARK: I did too.

LANG: How can you say that! He even carried you up four flights of stairs.

PARK: Well, I was carrying two suitcases at the time. Where's the bedroom?

LANG: Oh, no, John Bickerson. There's work to be done. You go in the kitchen and unpack that barrel of dishes.

PARK: Listen, Blanche, can't we do that in the morn—

LANG: No! You promised we'd get everything straightened out and—

PARK: Okay, okay, okay…(FADING)…Work like a horse all day, now she won't let me…

MAN: (FADING IN) Shall I set it down here, ma'am?

LANG: Oh. Yes, please—over in that corner…(LABORED FOOTSTEPS…BARREL IS SET DOWN HEAVILY)…That's everything isn't it?

MAN: Yes, ma'am. Two beds, two bureaus, three barrels, eleven suitcases, two trunks, four cartons, one crate, one table and four chairs, one radio, stove and refrigerator, nine cases of bourbon and one ice bag.

LANG: That checks with my list. How much do I owe you?

MAN: Nineteen dollars and seventy-five cents.

LANG: Oh, dear. All I've got is a twenty dollar bill. Have you got change?

MAN: No, ma'am. But I'll carry the stove down and bring it up again if you want me to work out the extra quarter.

LANG: Oh, never mind. Here, you can keep the whole thing.

MAN: Thanks. (FADING) Two bits for breaking my back—I should have been a bookmaker (DOOR SLAMS).

LANG: What a mess! Where in the world do I begin? I wonder if John could nail the pictures on the wall without disturbing the other tenants…John!…John!…(FOOTSTEPS) Where is that man?

SOUND: (DOOR OPENS)

PARK: (SNORES LUSTILY…WHINES)

LANG: How can he sleep in a barrel!

PARK: (SNORES AND GIGGLES MERRILY)

LANG: John! John, get out of that barrel!

PARK: (A PROTESTING WHINE) Mmmmm!

LANG: Get out, get out, get out!

PARK: Get out, Blanche! Wassamatter!…Whyncha lemmee sleep? Whaddya want, Blanche?

LANG: Get out of that barrel! I'll bet you've broken all my dishes.

PARK: Only one. Here.

LANG: What did you do that for? You broke the handle off my chafing dish!

PARK: Well, it was chafing me. Goodnight.

LANG: Don't you curl up in there again! Come on—you wake up and start unpacking these things!

PARK: Ohhhh! (GETS OUT OF BARREL) I don't know why I have—

SOUND: CRASH OF DISHES

LANG: John! More dishes?

PARK: No—less.

LANG: What's the matter with you? How can you be so clumsy!

PARK: I couldn't help it—they stuck to my overcoat.

LANG: You can't help anything! And why are you wearing that overcoat anyway? Nobody wears an overcoat in the middle of June.

PARK: I had to wear it.

LANG: What for?

PARK: Because I had to…here, hang it up.

LANG: John Bickerson!

PARK: Oh, quit staring and help me unhook my bourbon girdle.

LANG:	That is the most ridiculous thing I ever saw! Twenty-four bottles of bourbon hanging from a garter belt.
PARK:	Well, I wasn't gonna trust that moving man with my life's blood. Let's go to sleep, Blanche—I can't keep my eyes open.
LANG:	We can't go to sleep! You've got to put the beds up.
PARK:	I'll put 'em up in the morning. Crawl in the other barrel.
LANG:	You're insane. I'd smother to death.
PARK:	Stick your nose through the bunghole.
LANG:	Now you listen to me! Neither of us going to sleep until the whole apartment is in order. I still have to take inventory.
PARK:	Why? Why do you have to do it now?
LANG:	So I won't have to do it tomorrow. Take that pad and call off the things as I check them.
PARK:	Okay. A bunch of mustard greens, two cans of tomato juice, a pound of chicken gizzards, half a pint of cottonseed oil—
LANG:	That's my shopping list!
PARK:	Shopping list?
LANG:	Yes, I'm going to bake a cake.
PARK:	A cake! With chicken gizzards?
LANG:	Don't be silly. That's for the cat. Take the other— John! The cat!
PARK:	What about him?
LANG:	Where is he? He's lost and it's all your fault! I begged you to take care of him and see that he got here safely!
PARK:	He'll get here. They'll deliver him in the morning.
LANG:	How do you know?
PARK:	I put him in a sack and dropped him in the mailbox.
LANG:	John, you didn't!
PARK:	Oh, stop blowing your cork! I didn't put him in any mailbox!
LANG:	Well, don't scare me like that. You'd better go out and look for him, John.
PARK:	Blanche, I guarantee you that cat'll be here in the morning.
LANG:	What makes you so sure?
PARK:	Because I tied a label around his neck with our new address on it.

LANG: What good is that? He can't read.

PARK: I know he can't read! But people can read and somebody's bound to pick him up and deliver him—heaven forbid.

LANG: You hate that cat, don't you?

PARK: I don't hate him at all.

LANG: You do too!

PARK: I do not! I love the cat, I love the canary and I love you! I don't know which one of you I love the most!

LANG: If the house ever caught fire which would you save first? The cat, the canary or me?

PARK: Me. Now look, Blanche—let's just throw the mattress down on the floor and get some sleep…

LANG: I don't see how you can sleep anyway. Haven't you got any romance in your soul?

PARK: Blanche, it's almost two o'clock in the morning.

LANG: I don't care. For the first time since we got married we have a real home and you didn't even carry me across the threshold.

PARK: Carry you across the threshold! That's for newlyweds.

LANG: What of it? We've only been married eight years.

PARK: Well, I can't carry a grudge that long. Put out the lights, Blanche.

LANG: I don't understand you, I swear I don't. Aren't you even going to kiss me goodnight?

PARK: Again? I kissed you goodnight last night, didn't I?

LANG: Is it such a terrible chore to kiss your wife goodnight every night? Am I so distasteful to you? Does it hurt you to kiss me?

PARK: Don't feel a thing.

LANG: That's because you have no feelings at all! Here we are, our first night in a brand new apartment—just like a second honeymoon and you're acting like an old worn-out married man.

PARK: I'm not acting. Put out the lights.

LANG: I'd like to hear you say that to Gloria Gooseby.

PARK: Now don't start with Gloria Gooseby!

LANG: Believe me, if Gloria Gosseby had to ask you for a kiss you wouldn't say "put out the lights."

PARK:	She never has to ask for it and I always put out the lights! I mean, I hate Gloria Gosseby and I'd like to spend one night of my life without her!
LANG:	Oh, is that where you've been spending your nights?
PARK:	Now listen, Blanche—you promised when we got this new apartment you wouldn't beef anymore. What's the matter with you? Why are you carrying on like this?
LANG:	Well, I've got something to tell you.
PARK:	Well, tell me.
LANG:	If you give me a kiss I'll tell you.
PARK:	Tell me now and I'll kiss you later.
LANG:	You might not feel like kissing me later.
PARK:	I don't feel like kissing you now.
LANG:	You hate me, don't you?
PARK:	Oh, I don't hate you, Blanche.
LANG:	You do, you do, you do! Why don't you say you're sorry you married me?
PARK:	Because I'm not! Blanche, why don't you stop tormenting me?
LANG:	Am I the only wife in the world for you?
PARK:	You're the only wife in the world for me!
LANG:	You're lying. Swear.
PARK:	I swear I'm lying!
LANG:	What!
PARK:	I mean I'm not lying!
LANG:	I never expected the first night in our new apartment would be like this. I've been looking forward to this day for years.
PARK:	Well, if you'll just calm down and let me get some rest I'll be able to appreciate it.
LANG:	Don't you like the place, John?
PARK:	I love it. But how can I afford it? We're still paying rent on the other one?
LANG:	Oh, somebody's going to sublet it…John, I wonder why that newspaper fellow never showed up?

PARK: How should I know?

LANG: Well, don't bark at me! You've been grumpy ever since you came home tonight with that lump on your head. How you could bump it on the doorknob I'll never know.

PARK: I don't know, either...And I still don't know how you managed to get this apartment for a measly thirty dollars a month. We're paying fifty for that goat's nest we lived in. How did you do it, Blanche?

LANG: Oh, I just used my head. I'm not as stupid as you think I am, you know.

PARK: I'm sure you're not. Did you set the alarm clock?

LANG: Yes, I set it.

PARK: For six-thirty?

LANG: Four-thirty.

PARK: Four-thirty? Who gets up at four-thirty?

LANG: You do. You have to bank the furnace.

PARK: What are you talking about? This is an apartment house—the janitor banks the furnace.

LANG: You're the janitor.

PARK What?!

LANG: How do you think I got the apartment so cheap?

PARK: I won't do it! I won't do it, I tell you! You must be out of your mind! I work seventeen hours a day—I'm not going to come home and scrub the floors—and be a janitor! We're getting out of here, do you hear me? Tonight!

LANG: We can't leave here. They're bringing the piano tomorrow.

PARK: Piano? What piano?

LANG: Well, this is such a beautiful apartment and our furniture is so shabby—I went out and bought a piano.

PARK: (HORRIFIED) Oh, Blanche!

LANG: We have five years to pay for it and I only had to give them a hundred dollars down.

PARK: Where did you get a hundred dollars?

LANG: I took it from the sugar bowl you had hidden in the closet.

PARK: Blanche! That money was for my life insurance! They'll lapse my policy!

LANG: No, they won't. I wrote and told them to deduct it from the money they'll owe us when you drop dead.

PARK: Don't say that!

LANG: Well, you always say it!

PARK: I don't care what I say! How can you squander my hard-earned money like that? I deny myself everything! I've been sewing sleeves on your old drawers and wearing 'em for sweatshirts! For six months I've been walking around with a broken wrist to save on doctor bills! I never spend a nickel on myself!

LANG: You had your shoes shined yesterday.

PARK: What shine? I had my feet painted black! You cancel that piano, do you hear me! And I'm not going to stay here and be a janitor!

LANG: Wait a minute, John—don't be hasty. Just listen to reason.

PARK: I'm deaf.

LANG: I'll cancel the piano, but I must have this apartment, it's got an extra bedroom.

PARK: We don't need an extra bedroom. One bedroom is enough for the two of us.

LANG: John, you don't understand. It isn't always going to be just the two of us. I only found out today that in a few months we're going to have another mouth to feed.

PARK: Blanche! You mean...

LANG: Yes. My mother is coming to live with us.

PARK: Goodnight, Blanche.

LANG: Goodnight, John.

MUSIC: BICKERSON PLAYOFF

HOLBROOK: And now, here are John and Blanche Bickerson as Frances Langford and Lew Parker.

PARK: Say, Frances—How about you and your husband dropping in at my house tonight? I'm giving a little party.

LANG: Love to, Lew. What's the occasion?

PARK: It's my wedding anniversary.

LANG: Really? How long have you been married?

PARK: Eight years.

LANG: Eight years…Just like the Bickersons.

PARK: Yes, but that's as far as the resemblance goes. I can truthfully say that in all the time we've been married my wife and I haven't had one single argument.

LANG: That's wonderful. It amazes me that a happily married man can give such a convincing performance as John Bickerson. How do you do it, Lew?

PARK: I just act natural…Goodnight, Frances.

LANG: Goodnight, Lew…Goodnight, everybody.

MUSIC: THEME UP TO FINISH.

THE BICKERSONS SHOW #6 (1951)

PRODUCER:	PHIL RAPP
PRODUCT:	PHILLIP MORRIS
AGENCY:	BLOW
TAPED:	JUNE 29, 1951
BROADCAST:	JULY 17, 1951

ANNCR: Stand by for the Bickersons!

RECORD COMMERCIAL

THEME: PHILLIP MORRIS CALLS.

(APPLAUSE)

HOLBROOK: And now the makers of Philip Morris cigarettes bring you Frances Langford and Lew Parker starring in Phil Rapp's humorous creation "The Bickersons"! But first here is Lew Parker as Lew Parker.

INTRO TO SONG

SONG: LANG & ORCH

(APPLAUSE)

HOLBROOK: Now here are Frances Langford and Lew Parker as John and Blanche Bickerson in "The Honeymoon Is Over."

THEME: SOFT AND PLAINTIVE.

HOLBROOK: A minor accident can sometimes be a blessing in disguise. Witness the change in John Bickerson as he rushes to poor Blanche who is suffering from an ankle sprain.

LANG: John, dear.

PARK: What do you want now?

LANG: Don't be short with me, darling.

PARK: I'm not short—I'm exhausted. What do you want?

LANG: My ankle is killing me. You'd better call Dr. Hersey.

PARK: You don't need a doctor, Blanche. Your ankle will be fine once you get out of bed and walk on it.

LANG: I don't think I can walk on it, John.

PARK: How do you know till you test it? Go on—kick the cat a few times and see how it feels.

LANG: Oh, stop it! I should have called Dr. Hersey last night.

PARK: Blanche, I've done everything for your ankle that a doctor would have done. Didn't I sit up till two o'clock in the morning massaging it with chicken-fat?

LANG: Chicken-fat. You and your insane remedies!

PARK: What do you want from me, Blanche? I can't keep waiting on you hand and foot. If I'm late for work I'll lose my job.

LANG: You think more of your job than you do of me.

PARK: Blanche, I'm late—I stayed up half the night taking care of you—now I've gotta rush to the office and get some sleep. Work!

LANG: I heard you the first time. Why can't I call Dr. Hersey, John?

PARK: What do you want that horse doctor for? He can't help you.

LANG: He can, too. He took very good care of Louise Shaw when she had her baby, and he could do the same for me.

PARK: Blanche, aren't you expecting a little too much of a sprained ankle?

LANG: Don't be so funny. Doctor Hersey's a good doctor and you know it.

PARK: Fine doctor! No matter what's wrong with you he says, "Take two aspirins and call me first thing in the morning."

LANG: John, I wonder if you're jealous of Dr. Hersey?

PARK: I'm not jealous, Blanche. I'm just suspicious of a doctor who gets presents from an undertaker.

LANG: You'll be sorry if you don't let me call Dr. Hersey, John—I'm sure my ankle's broken.

PARK: I won't be sorry. I mean, your ankle isn't broken—there isn't even a bruise. I'm going, Blanche.

LANG: What about the cat?

PARK: What about him?

LANG: Did you fix him his breakfast?

PARK: No, I didn't fix him his breakfast. There's nothing wrong with his ankle—let him fix it himself.

LANG: Please, John—it'll only take a minute.

PARK: What'll I give him?

LANG: Just give him a dish of cottage cheese and mix in a couple of raw eggs.

PARK: Eggs! Blanche, why does the cat have to eat eggs at a dollar ten a dozen?

LANG: They're good for him. Eggs make his coat glossy.

PARK: These left-over enchiladas are good enough for him.

LANG: Will they make his coat glossy?

PARK: Yeah—they'll put a shine on his pants, too. Is there any other little thing you'd like me to do, Blanche? You want the windows cleaned, or something? I've got almost three minutes before I'm due at the office, you know.

LANG: I'll manage now.

PARK: Fine. (OPENS DOOR)

LANG: John.

PARK: What is it now?

LANG: I'm worried about the back door—the hinges are loose.

PARK: They're not loose. I fixed them with scotch tape this morning.

LANG: Well, that won't hold. And with you out of the house, I'm worried.

PARK: What are you worried about?

LANG: Suppose some prowler breaks in here, finds me and carries me off?

PARK: It'll serve him right. Goodbye, Blanche.

MUSIC: BRIDGE

SOUND: KNOCK ON DOOR

LANG: Come in. The door's open.

SOUND: DOOR OPENS AND CLOSES

LANG: Oh, hello, Clara.

CLARA: Blanche! Aren't you ashamed to still be in bed at two in the afternoon? I've been up an hour already.

LANG: I sprained my ankle last night. I can't walk.

CLARA: Oh, that's terrible.

LANG: It doesn't hurt too much now.

CLARA: Good. Then, could you go over and keep an eye on my kids while I'm shopping?

LANG:	What's the matter with you, Clara! I told you I can't get out of bed.
CLARA:	Oh. Well, as long as you're going to be in, I'll send the kids over here.
LANG:	No, you won't. I'm expecting Dr. Hersey any minute.
CLARA:	Dr. Hersey? Maybe I better leave before he comes.
LANG:	Why?
CLARA:	We don't use him anymore since he gypped us when little Ernie was born. Charged us $75.
LANG:	That doesn't sound unreasonable.
CLARA:	Ernie was no seventy-five-dollar baby, he only weighed four and a half pounds!
LANG:	My, that's almost as expensive as a rump roast.
CLARA:	Well, we never paid him. But, listen, Blanche, with you laid up like this, who's taking care of the house for you?
LANG:	John is.
CLARA:	It looks it!
LANG:	He'll manage fine when he's had time to straighten everything out. He's even coming home early to cook dinner for me.
CLARA:	Can John cook?
LANG:	You should see him.
CLARA:	All right, I'll bring Barney and the kids over at six.
LANG:	Well I didn't mean—-
CLARA:	It's no trouble. I told you a million times, Blanche, anytime my sister needs me I'll be there!
LANG:	Around dinner time…We'll see you then.
SOUND:	KNOCK ON DOOR
LANG:	Come in.
SOUND:	DOOR OPENS AND CLOSES
DON:	Well, now, little lady, what's happened to you?
LANG:	Oh hello, Dr. Hersey. You remember my sister Clara.
DON:	Indeed I do. Haven't seen you in some time, Mrs. Dollop. How are you?
CLARA:	Very well.

DON: And how is little Barney?

CLARA: You mean Ernie—Barney's my husband.

LANG: Excuse me for changing the subject, but would you pass me that glass of water, Doctor Hersey?

DON: Certainly.

LANG: Thank you.

CLARA: Ernie's fine. He's three now, you know.

DON: Yes, I know. Three years, two months and fifteen days to be exact.

CLARA: Quite a memory you've got.

DON: Not at all...I think back to it on the first of every month.

LANG: (CHOKES ON WATER)

CLARA: Well, don't stand there—you're a doctor—whack her on the back!

LANG: I'm all right—went down the wrong way. Clara, if you've got shopping to do, don't you think you'd—

CLARA: I was just leaving. Goodbye, Blanche.

LANG: Goodbye, Clara.

SOUND: DOOR OPENS AND CLOSES

DON: Now then, what's your problem?

LANG: Oh, I tripped on the stairs last night and hurt my ankle.

DON: You better let me have a look at it...Mmmm.

LANG: Pretty bad, isn't it?....Well, isn't it?

DON: No. I guess you're lucky. There isn't a thing wrong with it.

LANG: Of course there is. It hurts.

DON: Well, it may be a bit tender, but there's absolutely no damage. My advice to you is get up and walk around on it and you'll forget about it in an hour.

LANG: I don't want to forget about it. I mean—I think I'd better stay in bed for a day or two and give it a chance to heal.

DON: Well, you're the doctor.

LANG: Would you mind putting a bandage on it?

DON: Bandage?

LANG: Just so John feels he's getting his money's worth.

DON: Mm-hm. Hold your foot up.

LANG: You know, Doctor, I thought it was going to be heavenly spending a few days in bed, but, just between us, it's gotten a little dull already. Wish we had a television set.

DON: Say, now—that reminds me. They're delivering my new set today. I was going to trade in my old one, but—well, you can have it if you like.

LANG: Really? Oh, but we couldn't take it, Dr. Hersey.

DON: Why not? They're hardly giving me anything on a trade-in.

LANG: Well, I insist that we at least pay you what they offered on a trade-in.

DON: Well…If you insist.

LANG: It's a deal. How much did they offer?

DON: Seventy-three dollars and twenty-four cents. Call it seventy-three even.

LANG: Oh. Well, just add it to your bill for this call and send it to John's office.

DON: All right, Mrs. Bickerson…There…How does that feel?

LANG: Wonderful. Now it really feels like a sprained ankle.

DON: Yes. Well—I'll just write out this prescription and we'll be all through.

LANG: Oh, good…Then I'll have something else to show John.

DON: (AS HE WRITES) Really, Mrs. Bickerson—why do you need all these things to show John?

LANG: Well, you know John—he's the jealous type—and he didn't even want me to send for you.

DON: (WITH A TOLERANT CHUCKLE) Oh, I can't believe that he'd be jealous of me.

LANG: Well, he is. You should hear the things he says about you.

DON: What things?

LANG: Oh, all sorts of crazy things…Like "no matter what's wrong with a patient, you tell them to take two aspirin and call you in the morning"…And——Doctor Hersey! Why are you tearing up that prescription?

MUSIC: BRIDGE

SOUND: OFFICE NOISES…TYPING, ETC…DOOR OPENS AND CLOSES, TYPING STOPS

MAN:	Hello, Bickerson.
PARK:	Hello.
MAN:	Say, you really ought to start coming in earlier, fella—the old man's bound to notice it sooner or later.
PARK:	Did he come in yet?
MAN:	He just went out for lunch. How's the wife's ankle?
PARK:	Same way. I haven't slept a wink for five nights.
MAN:	Still can't walk, huh?
PARK:	Not a step. I'm getting housemaid's knee from waiting on her. Where's my samples?
MAN:	Under your desk. You going out on your route now?
PARK:	Yeah. Why?
MAN:	Nothing—only I wish you'd remember to take that apron off. You look like a Fuller Brush woman.
PARK:	How would you like a punch in the nose, Marvin?
MAN:	Just kidding, Bickerson—no need to get sore. Here's your mail.
PARK:	Throw it in the basket—probably just bills....Wait a minute! Let me look at those letters—might be something there from a Draft Board.
MAN:	You ain't that lucky. Here.
SOUND:	ENVELOPE BEING TORN OPEN...RUSTLE OF PAPER
MAN:	(AFTER SLIGHT PAUSE) You better pay that—they'll really shut off your lights, you know.
PARK:	Can't you keep your big nose out of my mail?
MAN:	Sorry.
PARK:	Here's one from my wife's doctor. Cheap buzzard couldn't even wait till the first of the month.
SOUND:	ENVELOPE BEING TORN OPEN...RUSTLE OF PAPER
PARK:	(READING) Enclosed find bill for Seventy——(DULL THUD)
MAN:	Bickerson! What happened? Bickerson—(SLAPPING SOUNDS) Talk to me! Don't move—I'll get you a little bourbon and water.
PARK:	(WEAKLY) Never mind the water.
MAN:	What's wrong? What happened?

PARK: One visit and that medical thief sends me a bill for 78 dollars. Seventy-eight dollars!

MAN: Take it easy, Bickerson.

PARK: That quack has no right to charge me 78 dollars! There's nothing wrong with my wife but a measly sprained ankle! Where's my hat?

MAN: What are you gonna do?

PARK: I'm gonna make him reduce this bill. No doctor's gonna charge me seventy-eight dollars for fixing my wife's ankle!

MAN: You can't bargain with a doctor!

PARK: Look, then I'll force him to take out her appendix!

MUSIC: BRIDGE

SOUND: PHONE RINGS...RECEIVER UP

DON: Hello?

LANG: (FILTER) Dr. Hersey, this is Blanche Bickerson. Did you send the bill to John's office like you promised?

DON: Yes, I did. Why?

LANG: Well, he hasn't mentioned it and I was wondering if he got it. Did you add on the 75 dollars for the television set?

DON: Certainly. (DOOR OPENS) You know you can trust me, Blanche...Oh, hello, Bickerson.

PARK: If that's my wife, I wanna talk to her.

DON: Oh, no—it's just a patient with a gallstone attack.

LANG: (FILTER) Hello?

DON: (INTO PHONE) Take two aspirin and call me back in the morning. (HANGS UP) Now what's on your mind, Bickerson?

PARK: I just got your bill.

DON: Well! And you promptly dropped in.

PARK: I nearly dropped dead!...Seventy-eight dollars! For what?? It isn't worth it!

DON: Now calm yourself, Bickerson. It isn't a lot of money when you consider the entertainment values.

PARK: What?

DON: That seventy-eight dollars entitles you to many an evening's fun.

PARK: What's that got to do with you?

DON: Look here, Bickerson—anytime you're bored and think it's too expensive I'll be glad to relieve you of your burden.

PARK: Now it comes out! I never did trust you, Hersey.

DON: I don't see what you're complaining about, Bickerson—you got the best part of the bargain. That's no hunk of junk sitting in your bedroom, you know.

PARK: Well, thanks!

DON: Maybe a little banged up in spots, but on the whole in fairly good condition. Those legs are handrubbed.

PARK: Nobody asked you to rub 'em!

DON: Maybe not, but it makes them last longer. I suppose you'd rather I left the job for you.

PARK: Yes, I would!

DON: Well, there's still plenty to do if you're so ambitious.

PARK: There is, huh?

DON: Yes. How about a good shellacking?

PARK: How would you like a good shellacking?

DON: Oh, I've had enough of this, Bickerson. If you don't like the television set, bring it back.

PARK: If I don't like the what?

DON: The television set I sold your wife—the one with the handrubbed legs.

PARK: So that's why the bill was 78 dollars.

DON: Didn't Mrs. Bickerson tell you about it? I guess she's saving it for a surprise.

PARK: Yes. That little devil.

DON: Oh, you're going to really enjoy that television set. And you got it just in time.

PARK: I did, huh?

DON: Yes…I understand there's going to be a big fight tonight.

PARK: You can count on that, Doc.

MUSIC: BRIDGE

BICKERSONS

HOLBROOK: (CHUCKLES) In a moment, we'll join the "happy" Bickersons. Right now, it's time to join our roving reporter, Jay Jackson, for the story of his interview with an actual smoker in Memphis, Tennessee. Okay, Jay Jackson!

(SWITCH TO INTERVIEW)

RECORDING

JACKSON: Hello there. This is Jay Jackson. While we've been setting up our microphones here in the beautiful lobby of the Hotel Peabody in Memphis, Tennessee, my assistant has located a volunteer to try the Philip Morris Nose Test. How we doing, Frank?

FRANK: All set, Jay. Jay, I'd like you to meet Mr. Wick Richardson of Memphis, Tennessee. Mr. Richardson is not a Philip Morris smoker.

JACKSON: Thank you, Frank. How do you do, Mr. Richardson.

RICHARDSON: How do you do.

JACKSON: Now, about this test, I'd like to ask you one favor first. Please, for obvious reasons, do not refer to your present cigarette by its brand name. All right?

RICHARDSON: I see.

JACKSON: Okay. All right, Mr. Richardson, now let me give you a Philip Morris cigarette.

RICHARDSON: Thank you.

JACKSON: There we are. And do you have one of your own brand handy?

RICHARDSON: I do.

JACKSON: Good. Now, sir, which of the two cigarettes would you prefer to light first?

RICHARDSON: I'll light your cigarette first.

JACKSON: The Philip Morris first. All right, sir, let me light it for you, then I want you to take a puff, do not inhale, and let the smoke come slowly through your nose. That's the idea. That was the Philip Morris first—right, sir?

RICHARDSON: Right.

JACKSON: Now, Mr. Richardson, let's try exactly the same test with your own cigarette, which I notice is also one of the leading brands. I'll light it for you, you take a puff, do not inhale, and let the smoke come slowly through your nose. There we are. Now, sir, you've tried exactly the same test with both cigarettes—first with the Philip Morris and then with your own brand. Right?

RICHARDSON: Right.

JACKSON: Tell me, Mr. Richardson, what difference, if any, did you notice between the two cigarettes?

RICHARDSON: The Philip Morris doesn't burn as much.

JACKSON: You found the Philip Morris didn't burn as much as your own brand.

RICHARDSON: That's right.

JACKSON: Well, Mr. Richardson, you've just confirmed the judgement of thousands of other smokers all over the country who've also found that Philip Morris is milder. Thank you very much.

END OF RECORDING

HOLBROOK: Remember this…the test you just heard is entirely voluntary and no payment whatsoever is made for any statement in the interview. Yes, try this test—BELIEVE IN YOURSELF—and you too will believe in PHILIP MORRIS, America's FINEST Cigarette!

ANN: And now, back to Frances Langford and Lew Parker as John and Blanche Bickerson in "The Honeymoon Is Over."

THEME: (SOFT AND PLAINTIVE)

ANN: Well, John Bickerson threatened to bawl Blanche out and make her give up the television set, and that's exactly what happened. He threatened, she bawled, and he gave up.

It is now well past midnight, and the overworked John, who has spent five days as a household drudge in addition to his duties as a nightnurse for his invalid wife, has just gone to the drugstore for medical supplies. Blanche is on the telephone with her sister Clara. Listen.

LANG: Oh, it isn't so terrible, Clara. I needed the rest anyway. And John has been a perfect angel.

CLARA: Well, isn't that nice?

LANG: He doesn't growl anymore, and he's forever bringing home flowers. Honest, you'd think it was my funeral, he's so agreeable.

CLARA: Well, isn't that nice. My Barney's got more feeling than a rattlesnake.

LANG: Well, isn't that nice. I can hardly wait for John to get back, I've got some things for him to do.

CLARA: Oh, what did John say when he found out about the television set?

LANG: You only live two blocks away, didn't you hear him?

CLARA: He got mad, huh?

LANG: Only for a minute—but fortunately my ankle began to hurt and he shut up like a dear. I'd better get back in bed, Clara. John will be home any minute and I don't want him to know I can walk around. Maybe he won't be so nice to me.

CLARA: Well, don't be a fool and let on. Is your ankle black-and-blue?

LANG: It was but it's fading now. I have to keep knocking it with a heavy spoon....Oh, I hear him coming now! Goodnight, dear—I'll call you tomorrow. (RECEIVER UP...SCRAMBLES INTO BED...KEY IN LOCK...DOOR OPENS...CLOSES)

PARK: (MUTTERING) Ohhh—when am I gonna get some sleep?

LANG: (CALLING CHEERFULLY) Is that you, John?

PARK: Who were you expecting?

LANG: What?

PARK: Nothing. Here's the stuff...(DUMPS EVERYTHING ON TABLE) Gotta get my clothes off.

LANG: Where'd you pick up that filthy, wet bar rag?

PARK: It's not a bar rag—it's my shirt. I had to mop up the floor in the drugstore.

LANG: What happened?

PARK: I bent over to tie my shoelace and one of the straps broke on my bourbon holster.

LANG: John Bickerson! You didn't wear that thing down to the drugstore!

PARK: Who didn't?

LANG: I can't believe you put it on!

PARK: I never take it off. Where's the funnel, Blanche?

LANG: Funnel?

PARK: Yes, funnel! I wanna wring my shirt out in a bottle.

LANG: John, you're not really—

PARK: No. I'm just going to put the light out in the bathroom. (FOOTSTEPS...DOOR OPENS)

LANG: I better set the alarm. He has to get up so early, poor thing. (WINDS CLOCK AND SETS ALARM) Where's my bed jacket?...John!...John!...What's he doing in there? (CALLS—OFF) John!

PARK: (SNORES LUSTILY...WHINES...SNORES AND WHINES)

LANG: (OFF) John!

PARK: (SNORES AND GIGGLES)

LANG: I'll bet he fell asleep in the bathtub.

PARK: (SNORES AND GIGGLES MERRILY)

LANG: John! John Bickerson!

PARK: Mmm? Wassamatter? Wassamatter, Blanche?

LANG: Come on out of there!

PARK: Come outta there. (FOOTSTEPS) What happened?

LANG: You went in there to put out the light and you started snoring like a suction pump.

PARK: Put out the lights, Blanche. Goodnight.

LANG: Aren't you going to doctor me?

PARK: Blanche, there's nothing more I can do for your sprained ankle. Take an aspirin and go to sleep. I'm exhausted.

LANG: What did you do with the stuff from the drugstore, John?

PARK: It's on your night table.

LANG: You didn't bring everything.

PARK: Brought everything.

LANG: You got the liniment and the aspirin and the hot water bottle—but where's the elastic ankle bandage?

PARK: Isn't it there?

LANG: No.

PARK: Must have forgot it.

LANG: Go back and get it.

PARK: Can't. Drugstore's closed.

LANG: My ankle pains terrible.

PARK: I'll get you a bandage in the morning.

LANG: What good is that? How do I know it'll still hurt in the morning?

PARK: I'll twist it. Please, Blanche—you can get along without the bandage. Just let me get a couple of hours rest.

LANG: You poor thing. I'm sorry, John. You really must be exhausted.

PARK: Dead.

LANG: Do you want to go to sleep?

PARK: Yes.

LANG: All right, dear. Make me something to eat.

PARK: Eat! I made you something to eat an hour ago! I made you dinner two hours before that! You've been eating all night like you were condemned!

LANG: Don't shout at me—I'm an invalid.

PARK: Okay. What do you want?

LANG: I don't want anything.

PARK: I didn't mean to holler—I'm just tired. Shall I warm up those eggs again?

LANG: No. They were too hard and I can only eat soft-boiled eggs.

PARK: Well, I can't make 'em any softer. I boiled 'em for twenty minutes and they still didn't get tender.

LANG: Never mind. I'm not too hungry, anyway.

PARK: Can I go to sleep now?

LANG: Yes, dear.

PARK: Put out the light.

LANG: In a minute.

PARK: Blanche, what are you doing?

LANG: I'm fixing my face. I have to get ready for bed, don't I?

PARK: You've been in bed five days! Every night you cream your elbows, spray your chin, roll your neck—just when I try to get some sleep. Put out the lights.

LANG: I haven't finished my face yet.

PARK: Your face is finished.

LANG: No, it isn't. I have to let this greasepack set for ten minutes otherwise it has no effect.

PARK: Greasepack?

LANG: It's guaranteed to make you beautiful in five treatments. This is my fourth.

PARK: It is, huh?

LANG:	Yes.
PARK:	Boy, that fifth treatment must be a pip.
LANG:	Oh, that's too bad about you, John Bickerson! Maybe your other girlfriends don't have to use face cream.
PARK:	I had to open my big mouth!
LANG:	What a fool I am. I go thru torture to look good for you and you reward me with insults.
PARK:	What torture?
LANG:	I just wish you had to spend a whole day under a permanent wave machine—or have your eyebrows done.
PARK:	Why do you have to wave your eyebrows?
LANG:	I don't wave my eyebrows. I have them plucked.
PARK:	What for?
LANG:	Because it sets off my eyes and improves the lines of my face.
PARK:	Your eyes are offset enough—and you've got plenty of lines in your face. You don't have to pluck your eyebrows for me.
LANG:	Yes I do!
PARK:	You do not! I like 'em the way they are—nice and bushy!
LANG:	That's a left-handed compliment if I ever heard one!
PARK:	Well, I'm left-handed. Throw away that stuff and let me get some sleep!
LANG:	I noticed you never complain about Gloria Gooseby's make-up.
PARK:	Now don't start with Gloria Gooseby!
LANG:	She has to struggle out of twelve pounds of cosmetic before you can even get close to her.
PARK:	I always get close to her and she never struggles! I mean, I hate the sight of Gloria Gooseby and you know it!
LANG:	That's not true. You made an absolute fool of yourself the way you followed her around at her cocktail party.
PARK:	I wasn't following her, she was dragging me. She picked up a martini glass I hadn't finished yet.
LANG:	Oh, sure. I'll bet I could have the men tagging after me too if I could afford the clothes she wears.
PARK:	Your clothes are better than hers.

LANG:	That's what you say.
PARK:	If you wanna know something the dress she wore that night had a big rip in it!
LANG:	Oh, you were seeing things!
PARK:	I know—but she wore it just the same. Now put out the lights.
LANG:	Not until you promise to get me a new dress.
PARK:	Blanche, how can you even think of new dresses after the way you've been squandering my money.
LANG:	I don't spend a penny except on the bare necessities.
PARK:	Since when is a broken-down television set a bare necessity?
LANG:	Well, it was a bargain.
PARK:	Seventy-five dollars for that piece of junk!
LANG:	It's not a piece of junk. It's practically brand-new and it has the Giant, Life-Size Three-Inch Screen.
PARK:	If you had to have a television set, why couldn't you buy a decent one—with a 20-inch screen?
LANG:	What would we do with a 20-inch screen in a 19-inch apartment?
PARK:	I don't know, and I don't care. How much longer you gonna be with that greaseball, Blanche? I must get a few minutes sleep.
LANG:	I'm finished now. Goodnight, John.
PARK:	Goodnight.
LANG:	It wouldn't hurt you to kiss me goodnight, you know.
PARK:	It hurts.
LANG:	Funny how seven years of marriage can change a man.
PARK:	Mmmm.
LANG:	Before we were married you'd stand in my living room every night and pucker your lips the minute I came in. Why don't you do it now, John?
PARK:	Because I'm too pooped to pucker.
LANG:	See! You're beginning to get crotchety again! I knew it couldn't last!
PARK:	Blanche, what do you want? I've done everything a human being could! Why don't you let me sleep?
LANG:	I want to ask you a question, John.

PARK: In the morning.

LANG: No, tonight. If I die from this sprained ankle, will you marry again?

PARK: Not tonight.

LANG: Why don't you answer me, John? Will you ever marry again?

PARK: Never! I hope my nose drops off if I ever marry again!

LANG: If you had it to do all over would you marry me?

PARK: Sure. If I had to.

LANG: Are you sure I haven't been too much of a bother for you?

PARK: No bother.

LANG: You've been awfully sweet.

PARK: Mmm.

LANG: And you're not angry because you've had to cook for me?

PARK: No—just go to sleep.

LANG: Well, I don't want to be a burden to you, John.

PARK: No burden.

LANG: You've been so affectionate up to now and you seemed to have changed.

PARK: No change.

LANG: Do you love me still?

PARK: I don't know—I never saw you that way.

LANG: Well, just tell me that you——

PARK: Listen, Blanche, I'm not gonna tell you anything. I have to get up at the crack of dawn and wait on you because you can't walk—then I have to go to—(PHONE RINGS)—is that the phone?

LANG: I'll get it, dear…(LEAPS OUT OF BED…RUNS…RECEIVER UP) Hello?….(BUZZ)…Hello….(BUZZ FROM DEAD LINE) That's funny—there's nobody on the line…(HANGS UP) Wonder who it was…(WALKS BACK TO BED) Why are you staring at me like that, John?

PARK: I thought you couldn't walk.

LANG: Walk?

PARK: Yes, walk! How come you leaped out of bed like an acrobat! I thought you had a sprained ankle!

LANG:	Are you angry with me, John?
PARK:	Yes, I'm furious! What kind of a dirty trick is that!
LANG:	Go on—hit me with a heavy spoon!
PARK:	Why did you pretend to have a sprained ankle?
LANG:	Well, I just wanted a little sympathy from you.
PARK:	Blanche, you're the most selfish woman in the world—you're always killing yourself to get my sympathy. Last year you had your adenoids removed—six months ago you had your tonsils taken out—two weeks ago you had five teeth pulled—you'll run out of parts before I run out of sympathy!
LANG:	I'm sorry, John.
PARK:	What a trick! I ought to take you and—
LANG:	Don't you dare threaten me, John Bickerson! I'm entitled to a little rest, too. I work just as hard as you do and I never have any pleasure at all.
PARK:	Okay, okay.
LANG:	I'm fed up with the way you carry on over every little thing! What harm have I done? Just because I turned you into a human being—
PARK:	Okay! Let's go to sleep and forget about it!
LANG:	No, we won't! I'm going to give you a piece of my mind! You've had it coming to you for a long time. You think you're the only one who—oh! Ohhh!
PARK:	What's the matter?
LANG:	(SPEAKING WITH DIFFICULTY) My jaw. I can't talk.
PARK:	You can't talk?
LANG:	Nh-nh.
PARK:	Lie still—don't touch it. (HE SCRAMBLES OUT OF BED) I'll call Dr. Hersey. (LIFTS RECEIVER AND DIALS) Don't be scared, Blanche—I'm sure it's only temporary.
DON:	(FILTER) Hello?
PARK:	Dr. Hersey? This is John Bickerson.
DON:	Yes?
PARK:	I think my wife has dislocated her jaw—she can't talk.

DON:	She can't move her jaw at all?
PARK:	No. If you're in the neighborhood sometime next week you might drop in! Goodnight. (HANGS UP...GETS BACK IN BED) Goodnight, Blanche.
LANG:	Goodnight, John.
PARK:	Oh, what's the use!
MUSIC:	BICKERSON PLAYOFF
	(APPLAUSE)
HOLBROOK:	Now here are John and Blanche Bickerson as Frances Langford and Lew Parker.
PARK:	Say, Frances, how are you coming along with your new picture?
LANG:	Fine, Lew. Have you signed for one yet?
PARK:	I was just going to tell you about that. Happened all because of this radio program, too. Last week my wife was visiting a movie producer friend of ours and she made him tune in our show. Right after the broadcast my wife called me with the good news.
LANG:	Lew! You mean—
PARK:	Yep—she starts working tomorrow. Goodnight, Frances.
LANG:	Goodnight, Lew. Goodnight, everyone.
	(APPLAUSE)
HOLBROOK:	Thank you, Frances and Lew for the curtain call. And for America's FINEST Cigarette, here's another call well-worth remembering…
JOHNNY:	CALL…. FOR…PHILIP…MORRIS.
MUSIC:	"ON THE TRAIL" THEME
JOHNNY:	CALL…FOR…PHILIP…MORRIS! CALL…FOR…PHILIP…MORRIS.
MUSIC:	THEME UP
	(APPLAUSE)
HOLBROOK:	Be sure to listen next Tuesday night when PHILIP MORRIS again will present The Bickersons. And don't miss the PHILIP MORRIS Playhouse this coming Thursday night over this same station when PHILIP MORRIS will present Dan Duryea and Lucille Watson, starring in "Night Must Fall." That's Thursday night for the PHILIP MORRIS Playhouse, over CBS. In the meantime, don't forget to…

JOHNNY: CALL...FOR...PHILIP...MORRIS!

MUSIC: OUT

(APPLAUSE)

HOLBROOK: The Bickersons came to you, transcribed, from Hollywood, California. John Holbrook speaking.

This is CBS...THE COLUMBIA BROADCASTING SYSTEM.

THE BICKERSONS SHOW #9 (1951)

PRODUCER: PHIL RAPP
PRODUCT: PHILIP MORRIS
AGENCY: THE BLOW CO., INC.
BROADCAST: JULY 31, 1951

HOLBROOK: Ladies and gentlemen, Mr. Court Benson.

RECORDING

BENSON: Good evening, ladies and gentlemen. I have been asked to speak to you about radio and television commercials. I am sure that, like millions of other listeners, you have often found yourself bored and annoyed, and sometimes even angry at the commercials you hear...*bored* with the jingles, *annoyed* with the fancy phrases and wild claims, and *angry* with the sponsor for passing off fictitious surveys and paid testimonials instead of the simple facts about his product.

This has been especially true of cigarette commercials.

I think you will be pleased to know that in the program that follows, in a moment, there will be no ballyhoo, no singing sales talk, no attempt to make up your mind for you.

You will simply get the facts about the sponsor's product—and you will be asked to judge those facts for yourself.

This sponsor is...*PHILIP MORRIS*. All they ask is that you compare, match and judge PHILIP MORRIS against any other cigarette. And then, BELIEVE IN YOURSELF and *decide* for yourself which cigarette you prefer.

(MORE)

HOLBROOK: For the past four days, the Bickersons have been entertaining Blanche's sister Bertha as a house guest in their spacious one-room apartment. John has been sleeping on a cot in the kitchen and as we look in on them now it is seven in the morning and Blanche has just entered her husband's boudoir.

LANG: Well, it's about time you got up.

PARK: Mmm.

LANG: Don't just stand there scratching yourself, fold your cot up so I'll have room to make breakfast.

PARK: Fine place to sleep—on a cot in the kitchen.

LANG: What's wrong with it?

PARK: There isn't room enough in here to swing a cat.

LANG: You leave the cat alone. There's plenty of room in here.

PARK: There is not.

LANG: There is too. If you had put the breakfast table on top of the refrigerator, and the canary cage in the washing machine, then you could have shoved the stove in the doorway and had plenty of room for your cot between the sink and the cat's sandbox.

PARK: I tried that. The cot's too short—my head lopped over into the sink, and that leaky faucet kept dripping on my scalp.

LANG: Well, you should have worn a shower cap. (WIPING AND STACKING DISHES) John, you'll be late for work—when are you going to get dressed?

PARK: As soon as you've finished wiping the dishes with my shirt.

LANG: Oh. Well, you shouldn't have hung it on the towel rack. What do you want for breakfast?

PARK: Anything.

LANG: No, you've got to tell me exactly what you want. Then you won't have any complaints.

PARK: All right—fry me a couple of eggs.

LANG: I haven't got any eggs, you'll have to take cereal.

PARK: Forget it, Blanche…I'll get something to eat on the way to work.

LANG: If you'd have gotten up earlier my sister Bertha could have had a bite to eat before leaving the house.

PARK: She ate plenty. She was in here four times during the night for a snack.

LANG: So what? She didn't disturb you, did she?

PARK: Not much. She left the refrigerator door open and I woke up with frostbitten feet! Woman eats like a boa constrictor.

LANG: Bertha doesn't eat because she wants to—she was just trying to get rid of her heartburn. A lot you care how she suffers while you sleep.

PARK: Sleep? I didn't close my eyes all night.

LANG: Why not?

PARK: I was afraid we'd run out of food and she'd start in on me!...Where's my shoes?

LANG: You're wearing them. A fine one you are to talk about other people stuffing themselves—a man who can't even see his own shoes anymore. (MOVES POTS ON STOVE) You want your fried mush now?

PARK: No—and stop using my pants for a pot-holder!

LANG: Well, that's what you use them for!

PARK: Leave my pot out of this. I don't eat half as much as your fat sister.

LANG: You stop calling her fat, Bertha is a glandular case. Dr. Hersey says she's an ectomorph with overactive thyroids.

PARK: I don't care if she's a convertible with hydramatic drive—what'd you invite her to stay here for?

LANG: I told you we were having a family reunion. All my sisters are getting together. Clara and Barney arranged the whole thing.

PARK: Then why didn't Bertha stay with Clara and Barney?

LANG: They left town when they found out she was coming.

PARK: I thought so.

LANG: I don't mean that they left because she was coming—Barney had to go to Las Vegas on business.

PARK: What business? He hasn't worked in twelve years.

LANG: Well, he had a chance to collect unemployment insurance in Nevada. But they'll be back in time for the reunion. All my sisters will be here. Bess, and Vera, and Florrie and her family, and—

PARK: How many sisters have you got?

LANG: Seven. My mother doesn't like boys, so she never had any.

PARK: You talk like she had a choice in the matter.

LANG: My mother's a very strong-willed person, I'm sure she could have whatever she wanted.

PARK: Well, as far as I'm concerned she can have Bertha—and the sooner the better.

LANG: What have you got against Bertha?

PARK: Not a thing. I like her. She's just too big a woman for so small an apartment. And another thing—is she nuts? Why does she have to take forty baths a day?

LANG:	Oh, you're just not used to having a clean woman around the house.
PARK:	If she's going to be in that bathroom all the time why don't you give her the cot and let her sleep in there?
LANG:	In spite of what you say she's been very cooperative. She cooked dinner for us three times.
PARK:	That's another thing. What was that mess she whipped up last Saturday?
LANG:	What do you mean—mess? That was a delicious stewed rabbit.
PARK:	Are you sure?
LANG:	Of course I'm sure. What are you hinting at?
PARK:	Nothing—only I haven't seen the cat for three days.
LANG:	I had to send Nature Boy away to the Vet's after he bit Bertha.
PARK:	(DELIGHTED) He bit Bertha?
LANG:	It was some misunderstanding over a can of Puss and Boots. She was preparing it for him and he thought she was trying to eat it herself.
PARK:	She probably was.
LANG:	John Bickerson—why do you keep carrying on like this about my sister Bertha?
PARK:	Because I'm fed up, Blanche! Sleeping in the kitchen...Locked out of my own bathroom! I've had enough! I've got forty customers to see today, but do you think I'm in any shape to sell them?
LANG:	What kind of shape do you have to be in to sell bowling balls?
PARK:	Never mind the wisecracks, Blanche, I'm not putting up with it another night. When I come home this evening I want to find your sister Bertha gone!
SOUND:	DOOR OPENS
LANG:	But John—!
PARK:	It's her or me!
LANG:	(TEARFULLY) How can you act this way, John, when Bertha has been so sweet to us? Why she's probably out this very minute buying us a going away present.
PARK:	Just let her go away—that'll be present enough for me!
SOUND:	DOOR SLAM
MUSIC:	BRIDGE

LANG:	Hello, Bertha. Did you have a nice shopping trip?
BERTHA:	Didn't you make my bed yet, Blanche? It's almost five o'clock.
LANG:	I haven't had time, Bertha. I had to get dinner ready, you know.
BERTHA:	Well, don't feel bad about it, dear. If you can stand a sloppy apartment, I can too. Were there any calls for me?
LANG:	No.
BERTHA:	Well, don't let me interrupt your cooking. You go ahead and fix us a snack while I call home and see if anything is wrong.
LANG:	What can be wrong? You called home twice this morning.
BERTHA:	I know, Blanche, but my husband worries if he doesn't hear from me every couple of hours. He's not like John, you know.
LANG:	That's a fine thing to say! In the four days you've been here you've called him sixty times and he hasn't called you once.
BERTHA:	Well, you know Willie—he's just trying to keep the phone bill down.
LANG:	Well, so am I…Listen, Bertha, if you're so worried about your family why don't you——
BERTHA:	Have them come here? Don't be silly, Blanche. Your little dinky apartment isn't even big enough for the three of us. You know, it hurts me to see poor John sleeping in the kitchen.
LANG:	It hurts him, too.
BERTHA:	Well, it isn't my fault. If you remember, I was the one who suggested moving to a hotel when I saw how crowded we'd be. But John wouldn't move, would he?
LANG:	I don't think it's John's place to move, Bertha. After all, it's his apartment and the rest of our sisters are staying at hotels.
BERTHA:	Listen, Blanche—you're hinting about something. I can hear it in your voice.
LANG:	I'm not hinting. I—
BERTHA:	If you want me to move, come right out and say it. Don't be embarrassed. It won't mean a thing to me. Honestly.
LANG:	Well, since you put it that way…
BERTHA:	Please, Blanche—don't beat about the bush. We're blood relations. You can tell me, I won't get mad. Would you like me to move?
LANG:	Yes.
BERTHA:	How did I ever get such a snake for a sister????

LANG: Bertha!

BERTHA: Oh, I'm not mad at you, darling. I know it wasn't your idea. You're too fine and sensitive. It was that stupid husband of yours, wasn't it?

LANG: (TEARFULLY) Yes.

BERTHA: There, there. I knew you wouldn't have the brains or courage to suggest such a thing.

LANG: It isn't John's fault either that he's irritable. He hasn't sold anything in weeks, and that boss of his makes him miserable.

BERTHA: What's John's office number?

LANG: It's on the pad. What are you going to do?

BERTHA: Well, after all—I've been his guest for four days—he's married to my youngest sister—what sort of person would I be to leave without speaking to him?

LANG: Oh.

BERTHA: The least I can do is call him up and tell him to drop dead!

MUSIC: BRIDGE

SOUND: OFFICE NOISES...TYPING...DOOR OPENS...TYPING STOPS

MARVIN: Hello, Bickerson.

PARK: Hy'a, Marvin, ole boy! (SLAPS HIM ON THE BACK) Here— have a cigar. Nice day, isn't it?

MARVIN: Huh?

PARK: Oh, yeah...Here's the four bucks I owe you—and here's an extra buck for lending it to me.

MARVIN: Oh-oh. You better lower your voice, Bickerson—you want the old man to know you're crocked?

PARK: What are you talking about? Can't a guy be happy without being accused of being loaded?

MARVIN: Not you. The last time I saw you happy is when you got a draft notice by mistake.

PARK: Is that so? Well, feast your eyes on these orders, wise guy. (RUSTLES PAPERS)

MARVIN: (WHISTLES) How did you ever sell that many bowling balls?

PARK: Salesmanship, my boy.

MARVIN: Is this one on the level? Did you really sell 32 gross to an Old Ladies Home In Pasadena?

PARK: Sure. I convinced them it was good occupational therapy.

MARVIN: Occupational therapy! Those poor old ladies—it'll kill 'em!

PARK: They're not gonna bowl with 'em, silly. They're gonna string 'em together—they think they're beads!

MARVIN: Boy—that's really selling.

PARK: That's nothing. I got every pawnshop in town hanging three of our bowling balls over their doors...And you remember that civil war cannon in front of the Armory?

MARVIN: Yeah.

PARK: Next time you examine the cannonballs you'll discover that every one of 'em has two holes in it.

MARVIN: Our bowling balls! How'd you do it, Bickerson?

PARK: Simplest thing in the world...I suddenly realized that the toughest thing in the world to sell a bowler is a bowling ball. If he's a bowler, he's already got a bowling ball.

MARVIN: That's logical.

PARK: So I decided to concentrate on other uses for bowling balls...I tell you, there's a vast untapped market. I even got a scheme how to sell our lightweight two holer two at a time.

MARVIN: How?

PARK: Earrings. Before I'm through every woman in America will have our bowling balls hanging from her ears.

MARVIN: Bickersons—you're a cinch to get a raise for this.

PARK: Don't I know it. The minute I finish filing these orders I'm going in and talk to the old man.

MARVIN: Oh, by the way—some dame called here for you when you were out.

PARK: (PLEASED) Dame, huh? What'd she sound like?

MARVIN: She sounded like she wanted to kill you.

PARK: Oh, that was probably my wife. I'll be in my office, Marvin—let me know if the old man comes out.

MARVIN: Okay, Bickerson.

SOUND: DOOR OPENS AND CLOSES...TYPING RESUMES...DOOR OPENS...TYPING STOPS

MAN:	Marvin! Are you busy?
MARVIN:	No, Mister Striker.
MAN:	Well, why aren't you?
MARVIN:	Oh…Well, I thought you wanted something, sir.
MAN:	I do. Run downstairs and get me some aspirin—my head is splitting.
MARVIN:	Yes, sir.
SOUND:	PHONE RINGS
MAN:	You go ahead—I'll get it. (RECEIVER UP) Hello?
BERTHA:	(FILTER) Is that you, Stupid?
MAN:	What!
BERTHA:	I want to talk to John Bickerson and make it snappy.
MAN:	Who is this?
BERTHA:	It's his sister-in-law, Nosey. Now waddle over and call him to the phone.
MAN:	(ICILY) Listen, madam—I'm Bickerson's employer and I'm not used to being spoken to this way.
BERTHA:	Oh, so you're his boss, are you?
MAN:	That's right.
BERTHA:	Well, what do you expect me to do—bow to you over the phone?
MAN:	Now look here you—you—
BERTHA:	Don't threaten me, Buster—I know all about your vile temper.
MAN:	Oh, you do, eh?
BERTHA:	Yes, I do. I've been living at John Bickerson's house for four days and he told me what a miserable, mean, cheap old conniving four-flusher you are. He said that—
MAN:	I've heard enough! (SLAMS RECEIVER…DOOR OPENS)
PARK:	Oh, there you are, Mr. Striker. I—
MAN:	Bickerson—you're fired!
PARK:	Huh?
MUSIC:	BRIDGE
HOLBROOK:	(CHUCKLES) In a moment, we'll join the "happy" Bickersons. Right now, it's time to join our roving reporter, Bob Pfeiffer, for

the story of his interview with an actual smoker in Louisville, Ky. Okay, Bob Pfeiffer!

(SWITCH TO INTERVIEW)

(RECORDING)

PFEIFFER: Hello there. This is Bob Pfeiffer. While we've been setting up our microphone here in the heart of Louisville, Kentucky, my assistant has located a volunteer to try the Philip Morris Nose Test. Are we all set, Frank?

FRANK: All set, Bob. Bob, I'd like you to meet Mrs. Ruth Knight from Louisville, Kentucky. Mrs. Knight is not a Philip Morris smoker.

PFEIFFER: Thank you, Frank. How do you do, Mrs. Knight?

KNIGHT: How do you do?

PFEIFFER: About the test, now…may I ask you a favor…for obvious reasons, I'd like you not to refer to your present cigarette by its brand name. Is that okay?

KNIGHT: That's all right with me.

PFEIFFER: Now, let me offer you a Philip Morris, Mrs. Knight. Do you have one of your own brand handy?

KNIGHT: Yes, I do.

PFEIFFER: All right, which one would you like to light first, Mrs. Knight? You make the choice.

KNIGHT: I'll light my own first.

PFEIFFER: Your own brand first. All right, I'll give you a light, then I want you to take a puff, but do not inhale, and slowly let the smoke come through your nose. That's the way, Mrs. Knight. Now, that was your present brand first…which I noticed was also one of the leading cigarettes. Now, let's try exactly the same test with a Philip Morris. I'll give you a light, then I want you to take a puff, but do not inhale, and slowly let the smoke come through your nose. All right, Mrs. Knight, by your own choice now, you tried your own brand first and then you tried the Philip Morris and you make exactly the same test each time. Now, what difference, Mrs. Knight, did you notice between the two cigarettes?

KNIGHT: Well, I do find, I believe, the Philip Morris is a milder cigarette. It seems to me that it is.

PFEIFFER: Philip Morris you found milder?

KNIGHT: I believe it is, yes.

PFEIFFER: Mrs. Knight, you've just confirmed the judgement of thousands of other smokers who've also found that Philip Morris is milder. Thank you very much.

KNIGHT: You're very welcome.

(END OF RECORDING)

HOLBROOK: Remember this...the test you just heard is entirely voluntary and no payment whatsoever is made for any statement in the interview. Yes, try this test—BELIEVE IN YOURSELF—and you too will believe in PHILIP MORRIS, America's FINEST Cigarette! (PAUSE) And now...The Bickersons.

THEME: (SOFT AND PLAINTIVE)

HOLBROOK: Well, Blanche Bickerson's plans for a family reunion have already proved costly for poor husband John. He has succeeded in getting rid of his unwanted house-guest, Blanche's sister Bertha, but the effort has cost him his job. It is now three o'clock in the morning, and Mrs. Bickerson grits her teeth in anguish as the unfortunate John, afflicted with a type of insomnia that defies medical science, gives audible proof of his suffering. Listen.

PARK: (SNORES LUSTILY...WHINES...SNORES AND WHINES... A BROKEN RHYTHM SNORE FOLLOWED BY A WHINE)

LANG: It's like sleeping with a one-man band.

PARK: (SNORES AND GIGGLES)

LANG: Oh dear.

PARK: (SNORES AND GIGGLES MERRILY)

LANG: John!

PARK: Mmm.

LANG: Turn over on your side. Go on!

PARK: (A PROTESTING WHINE) Mmmmmmmm.

LANG: Please, please, please! Cut it out!

PARK: Cut it out, Blanche...Wassamatter? Wassamatter, Blanche?

LANG: That whining and snoring and rasping and growling has kept me awake for three hours.

PARK: Me too, Blanche. Who's doing it?

LANG: You're doing it! I even called Dr. Hersey to listen to you snore over the phone. I was going out of my mind!

PARK: Wassamatter with you, Blanche? Calling doctors at three o'clock in the morning! Wassamatter with you?

LANG: I couldn't help it! Something had to be done, John. Who else could I tell that you've been snoring like a madman for months?

PARK: Madman Muntz!

LANG: Don't you be so funny, John Bickerson.

PARK: I'm not funny, Blanche. I'm sleepy.

LANG: I can't understand what's happened to you, John—you used to be so considerate. Since you got married to me you haven't got any sympathy at all.

PARK: I have too! I've got everybody's sympathy.

LANG: That's right, add insult to injury. Tell people I forced you into this marriage. Did I ever run after you?

PARK: Blanche, I wanna sleep.

LANG: Answer me! Didn't you hang around my house night after night bringing flowers and candy and heaven only knows what? Did I ever run after you?

PARK: Listen, a mouse-trap doesn't run after a mouse—but it catches him just the same!

LANG: How can you say such terrible things! I did everything I could to discourage you and you know it! Did I accept you the first time you proposed?

PARK: No.

LANG: Why not?

PARK: Because you weren't there!

LANG: I knew it! There's somebody else.

PARK: Oh, Blanche, there's nobody else.

LANG: I've been a trusting fool all these years. You stopped loving me the day you married me.

PARK: That wasn't the day at all!

LANG: What!

PARK: I mean I never stopped.

LANG: You don't act like you love me.

PARK: I act. Goodnight.

LANG: Then it's true—you don't love me.

PARK: Blanche, I love you! What do you want from me?

LANG: Why do you have to scream so! Why can't you tell me you love me, nice and quiet. Go on—say it.

PARK: I love you nice and quiet. Satisfied?

LANG: No, I'm not.

PARK: Listen, do I ever ask you to tell me you love me? Do I?

LANG: Maybe things would be a lot better if you did. Why don't you ask me once in a while?

PARK: All right—do you love me?

LANG: No. That'll teach you not to take so much for granted.

PARK: Oh, this is awful. Blanche, this is the first chance I've had to sleep since we threw your fat sister out of the house. Why don't you let me get some rest?

LANG: You'll get plenty of rest now that you've quit your job.

PARK: I didn't quit my job—your sister Bertha got me fired!

LANG: Don't change the subject. That job was no good anyway. You've had five jobs in the last five years, and one was worse than the other.

PARK: There was nothing wrong with any of 'em.

LANG: Not much. Who wants a husband who's a popcorn hustler? Or a fertilizer sifter? And the job you had before this one—a waitress checker.

PARK: A matress tester!

LANG: That's even worse. No regard for the future—you just grabbed any job that came along. What are you going to do now, John?

PARK: I don't know. I've been pounding my feet off all afternoon looking.

LANG: Did you find anything?

PARK: No.

LANG: That's the trouble with you—you're too darn choosy!

PARK: I'm not choosy! There aren't any jobs to be had.

LANG: I was waiting for you to say that. Well, I don't know where you've been looking, but I cut an ad out of tonight's paper… (RUSTLES NEWSPAPER) Listen to this: "Wanted Salesman. Age 35—45. Good salary and commission. Five-day week. Chance for advancement. Call Orchard 6-9241."…What's wrong with this job, John?

PARK:	Nothing—that's the one your sister got me fired from! Her and her big mouth!
LANG:	That's right, blame my poor sister. Go all over town and tell your friends that she got you fired.
PARK:	I'm not telling anybody anything!
LANG:	Just like a man. Blames a woman for his own miserable failings! Your boss has told me a dozen times that your mind wasn't on your work and you spent half the day at the office sleeping.
PARK:	That's because you keep me awake all night!
LANG:	I'd never bother you at all if it wasn't for your snoring.
PARK:	Can I help it if I snore?
LANG:	Yes, you can. Dr. Hersey says you snore because you have a pair of bulging polyps and they clog your antrum.
PARK:	Put out the lights.
LANG:	He says he can cure it with a very simple operation on your nose. Why don't you let him fix it, John?
PARK:	I'll go down there in the morning.
LANG:	You say it but you won't do it. Do it now!
PARK:	What!
LANG:	Go on—get up and let Dr. Hersey yank out your polyps.
PARK:	Are you out of your mind, Blanche? It's three o'clock in the morning and I'm not gonna let that medical thief chisel on my polyps.
LANG:	He doesn't chisel. He snips.
PARK:	I don't care if he whangs 'em off with a tire iron! Nobody's gonna lay a hand on my polyps. Now will you please let me close my eyes for five minutes?
LANG:	I'll bet you'd do it quick enough if you were married to Gloria Gooseby.
PARK:	Now don't start with Gloria Gooseby!
LANG:	She'd squeal her head off if you didn't do what she likes.
PARK:	I always do what she likes and she never squeals! I mean, I hate the sight of Gloria Gooseby, and I forbid you to mention her name again! Do you hear me?
LANG:	Yes, I hear you! And you keep your voice down. Do you want to wake little George?

PARK: Who's little George?

LANG: Florrie's baby.

PARK: Who's Florrie?

LANG: What's the matter with you, John? My sister Florrie from Peapack. Have you forgotten that Florrie and Osgood had a baby?

PARK: Are you talking about that hulking dollop that weighed seventeen pounds when he was born?

LANG: Sixteen! And he isn't hulking. He's three months old and he barely weighs eighty-seven pounds!

PARK: Eighty-seven pounds!

LANG: That's with his clothes on.

PARK: He only wears a diaper!

LANG: I told you to lower your voice…You'll wake him up.

PARK: How can he hear me in Peapack?

LANG: He isn't in Peapack—he's in the bathroom.

PARK: Bathroom? What's that elephant doing in my bathroom?

LANG: He's sleeping there. Florrie and Osgood are staying at a hotel tonight, but they're moving in here tomorrow.

PARK: What for? We just got rid of Bertha—what do we need with Florrie and her stupid husband?

LANG: They're going to keep me company while you're in the hospital.

PARK: What hospital? What are you talking about, Blanche?

LANG: Dr. Hersey has arranged everything. You're not working now and you've got the time. At eight o'clock in the morning he's going to operate on your polyps. I've even packed a bag for you.

PARK: What does that man want from me? Last week he wanted to shorten my uvula! Now he wants to snip my polyps. Who made this Dr. Hersey such an authority on snoring? What does he know about it?

LANG: Plenty. He's been doing it for twenty years.

PARK: What—snoring?

LANG: No, silly. Operating. He said you're not to have any solids after eight o'clock tonight. I hope you didn't eat when you came home.

PARK: I had some of that lemon meringue pie you made. I found it in the sink.

LANG: Lemon meringue pie? I didn't make any lemon meringue pie. That was an apple pie.

PARK: Well, what was that yellow stuff on top?

LANG: It got burned so I put unguentine on it.

PARK: Why didn't you throw it out? Why did you leave it around to poison me?

LANG: Now, don't go getting excited. Dr. Hersey said you're to get a good night's rest and be in a relaxed state for the operation.

PARK: Operations—Unguentine! Put out the lights.

LANG: Yes, dear. As soon as you give George his three o'clock feeding.

PARK: What?

LANG: His formula's in the kitchen. Warm it up and take it in to him. Go on, John—get up and feed the baby.

PARK: Nobody would believe this…(HE STRUGGLES OUT OF BED) Where's my slipper?

LANG: I didn't pack it in the bag. It's still under your pillow.

PARK: You packed everything else in there—why didn't you pack my slipper?

LANG: Well, I didn't know how soon you'd be walking.

PARK: Walking! I thought he was gonna operate on my nose?

LANG: He is—but you never can tell about complications.

PARK: What a life I lead! A short uvula, no polyps and one slipper!

LANG: Oh, hurry up and get George's formula before he starts to cry. And the cat's home again—careful you don't step on him.

PARK: (OFF) Where's his formula? I can't find any formula.

LANG: It's in the icebox. Right next to the flounder I bought for dinner.

PARK: (ON) There's no flounder and no formula. (GETS BACK IN BED) Put out the light.

LANG: Did you look in the yellow bowl?

PARK: I looked in the yellow bowl.

LANG: Well, what's in it?

PARK: Just the cat.

LANG: John Bickerson! Did that cat eat the flounder and George's food?

PARK:	I don't know. But he's sitting in the icebox picking his teeth with the bones and wiping his face with a diaper.
LANG:	That's terrible. What'll we feed little George?
PARK:	Feed him the cat.
LANG:	How can you be so heartless, John? The child has to be fed every half hour. He's wasting away.
PARK:	Wasting away. He weighs more than I do.
LANG:	I think I hear him yelping already. Go in there and rock him to sleep.
PARK:	I'll be glad to. Where's a rock?
LANG:	You stop talking like that. I'm responsible for that child and you'd better see that he's fed.
PARK:	What do you want me to give him, Blanche? The rest of that unguentine pie you made?
LANG:	Florrie sent over a half a dozen cans of baby food. Go on, get up and boil him some.
PARK:	I'll boil him. (GETS OUT OF BED...FOOTSTEPS FADING OFF) This is the night's rest I get before I go to the hospital to get my nose whacked off. (UP) Where's the stuff?
LANG:	(UP) On the kitchen table. And you needn't warm it or empty it into a dish. He's hungry enough to eat it as it is. Just take it to him in the can.
PARK:	(OFF...FOOTSTEPS) All right, all right!
SOUND:	(DOOR OPENS...CAN THROWN IN...FOOTSTEPS)
PARK:	(GETTING IN BED) Put out the lights.
LANG:	Have you gone crazy, John? What do you mean by throwing the can in there like that? How do you expect him to get at the food?
PARK:	There's a can opener on the wall.
LANG:	John Bickerson!
PARK:	Oh, please, Blanche. He isn't hungry and he isn't crying. He's in there sleeping like a horse!
LANG:	You didn't even look at him.
PARK:	I didn't have to look at him—I heard him snoring. Will you please let me get a little rest? I'll never be strong enough for the operation tomorrow.

LANG: Oh, don't be so dramatic about the operation. Thousands of people have operations every day. You wouldn't hear me carry on like that if I was going to have an operation.

PARK: Not much! You had to take ether to have glasses fitted.

LANG: Well, I'm very sensitive around the eyes. Anyway, the surgery you're going to have is not a bit serious.

PARK: Then why are you acting so jumpy?

LANG: Well, I'm worried about you, John. If anything did happen to you on the operating table it would all be my fault—so you know what I think?

PARK: I'd better not go through with it, huh?

LANG: No, I think you ought to make out a will.

PARK: Make out a will! I thought you were worried about me!

LANG: Well, you don't want to leave me at the mercy of all those grasping relatives of yours, do you? The minute you drop dead, they'll—

PARK: Don't talk like that! Can't you say pass on or something like that?

LANG: Well, you always say drop dead.

PARK: That's only when I'm talking about your brother-in-law!—You should be a little more delicate when you're discussing wills.

LANG: Why?

PARK: Because you make it sound like I'm gonna go any minute.

LANG: Well, they don't give you two weeks notice, you know. Every man should make out a will.

PARK: Listen, Blanche—I'm not making out any wills and I'm not going to the hospital.

LANG: You have to. I've already paid Dr. Hersey. He wanted forty dollars for the operation and ten dollars for the anesthetic.

PARK: I'll take the anesthetic, without the operation.

LANG: You're getting the operation without the anesthetic.

PARK: What!

LANG: I mean a real anesthetic. He's going to give you a local. Now be a dear and make out your will, John.

PARK: Blanche, how am I going to make out a will? I've got nothing to leave, anyway.

LANG:	You've got some stock, haven't you? Didn't you get some stock last year?
PARK:	Ten shares. Kentucky Saltpetre Mines. Preferred.
LANG:	My brother-in-law got you in on the ground floor, didn't he? Where is it now?
PARK:	In the ground. The whole thing isn't worth eight dollars and I want you to stop talking about making out wills! Let me get some sleep before I jump out the window!
LANG:	Now you've done it. George is awake.
PARK:	Who's George?
LANG:	The baby. You woke him up.
PARK:	I don't care! I didn't send for him!
LANG:	Well, you go get him. Bring him out and I'll take care of him. Go on, John—get George.
PARK:	(GETTING OUT OF BED) Oh, what's the use. Where's my slipper?
LANG:	You packed it back in your bag.
SOUND:	RUMMAGING THROUGH BAG
PARK:	What did you pack these lace curtains in here for?
LANG:	They're not lace curtains—those are your shorts. I made a mistake. Instead of draining them in Rinso, I rinsed them in Drano.
PARK:	Well, where's my other pair? Why didn't you pack those?
LANG:	I couldn't—the baby's wearing them. Florrie forgot to leave a change.
PARK:	(FADING OFF) You should have bought him something. (DOOR OPENS)
LANG:	I tried, but he wears an outsize diaper and they have to be made to order. Hurry up and wheel him out.
SOUND:	SQUEAKY CRIB WHEELED ON
PARK:	(FADING IN WITH SOUND) Three months old! Look at the size of him. He's built like a concrete grease-pit!
LANG:	He's a perfectly normal healthy baby. He can't help it if he's big. His mother and father are big.
PARK:	Big what?
LANG:	I think he's adorable.
PARK:	He looks just like Florrie. Turn him over and let me see his face.

LANG: That is his face.

PARK: Oh. Was this crib made to order for him?

LANG: Of course not. You can buy them anywhere for three-ninety-eight.

PARK: So that's little George.

LANG: Yes, and I'm going to have the pleasure of him all the time you're at the hospital.

PARK: Mmm.

LANG: Look at him lying there like a little cherub. So innocent in sleep. Soon he'll be walking and in a little while he'll begin to talk—he'll say such cute things…then his first day at school—he'll be so scared—maybe he'll be a wonderful scholar or a great athlete. He'll grow into manhood—handsome and strong. He might be a doctor, or a lawyer—he might even grow up to be the President of the United States. It makes you wonder, doesn't it?

PARK: (ABSENTLY) Uh-huh.

LANG: What are you thinking of, darling?

PARK: How can they make a crib like that for three-ninety-eight?

LANG: Goodnight, John.

PARK: Goodnight, Blanche…Goodnight, George.

MUSIC: PLAYOFF

(APPLAUSE)

HOLBROOK: In a moment Frances Langford and Lew Parker will return for a curtain call but first, may I make a friendly suggestion? You've heard the PHILIP MORRIS Nose Test. You've heard that PHILIP MORRIS is less irritating. Why not try that test. We believe you'll find that PHILIP MORRIS is not only less irritating but also more enjoyable…smoother…better tasting than any other cigarette. And now, once again here are John and Blanche Bickerson as Frances Langford and Lew Parker.

THE BICKERSONS SHOW #11 (1951)

PRODUCER: PHIL RAPP
PRODUCT: PHILIP MORRIS
AGENCY: THE BLOW COMPANY, INC.
BROADCAST: AUGUST 14, 1951

HOLBROOK: PHILIP MORRIS presents…from Hollywood,…"The Bickersons"…starring Frances Langford and Lew Parker.

MUSIC: THEME

JOHNNY: CALL…FOR…PHILIP…MORRIS!

MUSIC: (MUSIC UNDER)

VOICE: BELIEVE…IN…YOURSELF!

HOLBROOK: Yes, BELIEVE…IN…YOURSELF!! Compare PHILIP MORRIS—match PHILIP MORRIS—judge PHILIP MORRIS against any other brand! Then…decide for YOURSELF which cigarette is milder…tastier…more enjoyable. BELIEVE IN YOURSELF…and you'll believe in PHILIP MORRIS, America's FINEST CIGARETTE!

JOHNNY: CALL…FOR…PHILIP…MORRIS!

MUSIC: (THEME UP TO FINISH)

HOLBROOK: They fight, they yell, they squabble and squawk, but they love each other as much as any married couple in the world—that's Frances Langford and Lew Parker—stars of Philip Rapp's humorous creation—THE BICKERSONS. And here is John Bickerson himself—Lew Parker!

(APPLAUSE)

PARK: Thank you, ladies and gentlemen, and good evening. Before we get under way with our weekly Bickerson brawl, I'd like you to meet my lovely opponent in still another role. Here she is—the Purple Heart Girlfriend—Miss Frances Langford.

(APPLAUSE)

LANG: Thank you.

PARK: Frances, we've got a special request from the boys at Tucson Hospital. They'd like to hear you sing "_____".

LANG: I'd love to oblige Lew, so with the help of Tony Romano—this is for you fellows.

LANG: (SONG)

(APPLAUSE)

HOLBROOK: Friends, in a moment we'll have a look-in at the Bickersons…but first, I'd like to have a word with *the most important person in the world* when it comes to choosing a cigarette. That person, of course, is YOU. We of PHILIP MORRIS believe that no one's taste is more important to *YOU* than *YOUR* taste— no one's *judgement* is more important to *YOU* than YOUR judgement. That's why we ask you to…BELIEVE IN YOURSELF. That's why—unlike others—we of PHILIP MORRIS *never* ask you to test our brand alone. That's no *test* because it gives you *no choice*. We say…*compare* PHILIP MORRIS…*match* PHILIP MORRIS…*judge* PHILIP MORRIS against ANY OTHER CIGARETTE. Then make your *own* choice according to your own taste, your own judgement. In short BELIEVE IN YOURSELF. Later, you'll hear an interview with an actual smoker—not an actor, not a paid performer, but a real person—who will make the only fair cigarette test, the PHILIP MORRIS nose test. I know you'll be interested—so stay with us won't you? (PAUSE) Now, light up a PHILIP MORRIS…and let's join Frances Langford and Lew Parker as John and Blanche Bickerson in "The Honeymoon is Over."

THEME: (SOFT & PLAINTIVE)

PARK: Blanche! Blanche! (FOOTSTEPS) First time I've ever been hungry in the morning and she's not here to—Well, will you look at the way she's arranged the table! (TOUCHED) Silly romantic kid— Breakfast by candle-light! She's even got my cereal on the stove. Well, I won't wait for her to serve me. (SPOONS STUFF INTO BOWL…TASTES) Mmm—best she's ever made.

SOUND: DOOR OPENS AND CLOSES

LANG: Oh, I didn't think you'd be up yet, John. I just dashed out to get some eggs.

PARK: That's all right, honey.

LANG: You're not angry?

PARK: Of course not. Say, this breakfast-by-candle-light is wonderful, Blanche. Whatever gave you the idea?

LANG: The bulb blew out and I couldn't find a new one.

PARK: Oh.

LANG:	Stop stuffing yourself while I'm talking. What's that you're eating?
PARK:	Oatmeal.
LANG:	Oatmeal? Where'd you get oatmeal?
PARK	You ought to know. You left me a whole pot of it on the stove.
LANG:	That's the wallpaper paste! You promised to paper the bathroom this morning.
PARK:	How could I make such a mistake! I should have known it wasn't your oatmeal—it wasn't lumpy enough.
LANG:	Don't be so funny. That was the last of the paste. Now how are you going to put the wallpaper up?
PARK:	I'll lick it in place! Blanche, how can you worry about wallpaper when I'm practically poisoned!
LANG:	Oh, you're not poisoned—it's just flour and water. Now you just read your paper and I'll whip you up a nice omelette. (RATTLE OF PAN)
PARK:	I'm not hungry anymore.
LANG:	Don't be like that, John. I've already got the powdered eggs on—now all I have to do is chop up the turnips and peel the frog's legs. It's a wonderful dish.
PARK:	I'm not eating any powdered frog's legs!
LANG:	Well, what do you want me to do with it?
PARK:	Give it to the cat.
LANG:	You hate that cat, don't you?
PARK:	I don't hate anybody. I'm just getting tired of those outlandish dishes you keep making.
LANG:	What do you care? You never eat them.
PARK:	Can you blame me? Last week you made a seven-layer broccoli cake! And the week before you gave me a bowl of sheep soup! Whoever heard of sheep soup!
LANG:	That wasn't sheep soup. It was possum broth.
PARK:	If it's all the same to you, Blanche, I'll have my breakfast out.
LANG:	All right, dear. As long as you're going out would you mind dropping this bundle at the laundromat?
PARK:	I haven't time, Blanche. I'll be late.

LANG: Late for what? Didn't you tell me you weren't working this week?

PARK: That's right. But I've got another appointment.

LANG: Your appointment can wait. Let's sit down and discuss where we'll spend your vacation.

PARK: I'm not on a vacation! I've been laid off for a week!

LANG: Well, whatever you call it. Anyway, we both can use a rest.

PARK: Mmmm.

LANG: How would you like to go to Yellowstone National Park, John?

PARK: Fine. Where will you go?

LANG: What kind of a question is that?

PARK: Oh, Blanche—how can you think about vacations when I haven't even got carfare to the Unemployment Bureau?

LANG: If you made a decent living you could go there in a cab. You better start thinking about making some real money, John.

PARK: I make enough.

LANG: Oh, sure. You've been working seven years and you haven't even earned enough to file an Income Tax Return.

PARK: I have, too! Why, this year I even filed a claim for overpayment of taxes—and you know it, because I gave it to you to mail!

LANG: Well, I didn't mail it.

PARK: Why not?

LANG: Why should I spend three cents to tell the Government they owe you two cents?

PARK: Blanche, please—don't rile me up this morning. I've gotta keep my blood pressure down.

LANG: What's the matter with your blood pressure?

PARK: Nothing. I'll see you later, Blanche.

LANG: No. Wait a minute. Where are you going, John?

PARK: If you must know, I've got an appointment with the insurance doctor. He's gonna examine me for a policy.

LANG: Again? You were examined for insurance last week.

PARK: I have to go back for another check-up.

LANG: John! Is something wrong with you?

PARK: Well—

LANG: Don't hold anything back from me, dear. I'm your wife and I have a right to know. Why did they turn you down?

PARK: The doctor said I was sluggish.

LANG: Sluggish!

PARK: Yeah. I fell asleep twice while he was examining me with his stethoscope. He said my heart sounded like a freight train.

LANG: He was probably tuned in on your snores! There's nothing wrong with you, John. You have another policy, don't you?

PARK: Sure. I got it two months ago.

LANG: There! That proves you're healthy. How much is it for?

PARK: Fifty dollars.

LANG: Fifty dollars! That won't even pay for your funeral! I mean, that's an awful small policy. I've got the cat insured for more than that!

PARK: Well, they wouldn't give me anymore at the time. They said I was a bad risk. You know—sluggish.

LANG: That's ridiculous. How could they refuse insurance to such a husky-looking specimen. You go down there, John—you'll pass the test—you're in perfect health.

PARK: You really think so, Blanche?

LANG: Of course. And while you're down there have the doctor phone me. I want to talk to him about my insurance policy.

PARK: What's wrong with it?

LANG: Nothing, dear…I just want to change it and make my mother the beneficiary.

PARK: Your mother! What about me?

LANG: I can't take chances, John. At least I know she'll still be around to collect.

PARK: Goodbye, Blanche.

MUSIC: BRIDGE

LANG: Hello, Clara. Been waiting long?

CLARA: Only a few minutes, Blanche. I brought little Ernie along. He's over there in the corner poking around in the fuse box.

LANG: Won't he get a shock?

CLARA: If he does, I'll kill him! Let me give you a hand with that bundle.

LANG: Well, thanks, Clara.

CLARA: Listen, if sisters can't help each other out once in awhile, who can? Here—we can put your laundry in this machine.

(OPENS WASHING MACHINE DOOR)

LANG: No, wait—that one already has some laundry in it.

CLARA: Just a few things of Barney's and mine. Long as it costs a quarter why shouldn't we get the full benefit of it? (CLOSES WASHING MACHINE DOOR) There! Now put your quarter in.

LANG: Oh, all right. (PUTS QUARTER IN SLOT...MACHINE STARTS) Let's sit down over here.

CLARA: (AS WASHING MACHINE FADES TILL BARELY AUDIBLE) How's John been?

LANG: Same as ever.

CLARA: Sluggish, huh? He's been working too hard, Blanche! What he needs is a vacation.

LANG: He's got a vacation, but he won't go anywhere. He thinks we can't afford the prices in those resort hotels.

CLARA: What do you need a hotel for? Listen—Barney's brother Rudy from Oklahoma is motoring in today with his whole family for the grape picking season.

LANG: Rudy? Is he the brother with the twelve children?

CLARA: Yes, *you* remember—the baby's name is Herman.

LANG: That's the one with the long arms.

CLARA: Well, what do you expect? The kid's been picking grapes since he was weaned. Well, anyway, they're coming by trailer, and Barney says they'd like to rent an apartment and sell the trailer.

LANG: A trailer! Sounds exciting!

CLARA: You could go anywhere, and it wouldn't cost you a penny. I'm sure Rudy'll sell the trailer cheap.

LANG: Well...the only money I've got available is John's insurance money.

CLARA: Blanche, you know as well as I do John's much too sluggish to pass any insurance examination. You might as well help him enjoy that hundred and fifty dollars while there's still time.

LANG: Of course, a vacation would do us both a world of good.

CLARA:	Then it's all settled. I'll tell Barney to arrange a deal for the trailer with his brother Rudy. Now where's my little Ernie?
LANG:	(AS SOUND OF WASHING MACHINE FADES IN) I don't know—last I saw him he was sitting on my laundry just before you stuffed it into the washing machine.
CLARA:	Blanche! You don't think I could have—Oh, he'll be furious! I gave him his bath this morning!…Stop the machine!
LANG:	Oh relax, Clara. Ernie isn't in the washing machine, he's perfectly safe over there sitting on the counter.
CLARA:	Where?
LANG:	There—trying to cut his hair with that electric fan!
MUSIC:	BRIDGE
SOUND:	DOOR OPENS AND CLOSES
DOC:	Now then—Bickerson, isn't it?
PARK:	Mmmm.
DOC:	Did my nurse get your medical history in the waiting room?
PARK:	Mmm.
DOC:	As I recall, you were rejected on your last application for life insurance, is that correct?
PARK:	Mmm.
DOC:	And what was the medical diagnosis at that time?
PARK:	(SLIGHT PAUSE) Sluggish.
DOC:	Yes, of course. Can't understand why it slipped my mind. All right, let's have a look at you. Back, first…Hmmmmm. Now turn around. Hmmmmmm. Are you always as pasty-faced as this?
PARK:	Only after breakfast.
DOC:	How's that?
PARK:	This isn't one of my best days.
DOC:	Oh, I see.
PARK:	However, you don't have to hold my wrist, I can stand by myself.
DOC:	(SLIGHT PAUSE) I'm taking your pulse.
PARK:	Oh. Go right ahead.
DOC:	Hmmmmmmmmm.

PARK:	What is it, doc?
DOC:	Yes. Now—er—let me take your pulse once more while you step up and down on this chair. Ready—go.
SOUND:	STEPPING UP ON CHAIR AND THEN HEAVILY DOWN. TWICE.
DOC:	Oh my!!
PARK:	(PANICKY) What is it, Doc? Is it bad? You've got to tell me! I have a right to know!
DOC:	(COLDLY) You stepped on my foot.
PARK:	Oh. I'm sorry. Do you want to try it again?
DOC:	Rather not risk it. Your heart's clanking like an iron claw machine as it is.
PARK:	What are you wrapping that thing around my arm for?
DOC:	Just relax—want to get your blood pressure.
SOUND:	PUMPING UP BLOOD PRESSURE METER...PAUSE... THEN LETS AIR OUT
DOC:	Hmmmmmm.
PARK:	What is it, doc? Is it bad?
DOC:	Strange! For a man who's so sluggish, you've got the highest blood pressure I've ever recorded.
PARK:	I have?
DOC:	Do you drink?
PARK:	Well, thank you, doc—what've you got?
DOC:	I wasn't offering any—I'm trying to account for this high blood pressure.
PARK:	Oh. Well—yes, now and then I do have a drop of bourbon. At weddings—or other festive and aggravating occasions. Mostly when I lose my temper.
DOC:	Bickerson—the only way you'll ever get your blood pressure down enough to pass an insurance examination is to give up bourbon entirely.
PARK:	Give up bourbon entirely! How can you suggest such a thing, doc—I *hate* scotch!
DOC:	No scotch, either. You'll have to make a substitution of some sort.

PARK:	You mean like scotch?
DOC:	No. Whenever you feel that you're about to lose your temper, instead of taking a drink—eat something.
PARK:	Is this a joke?
DOC:	You want to be eligible for life insurance, don't you?
PARK:	I don't know. I'm not even sure I want to stay alive!
DOC:	Well, that's your problem. My advice is total abstinence.
PARK:	But, Doc—I've got two whole cases of bourbon at home. Can't I start this eating business after they're finished? Say next week?
DOC:	In your present condition I suggest that you pour that bourbon down the drain.
PARK:	All of it?
DOC:	Why not? After all—you can't take it with you when you go.
PARK:	Doc, if I can't take it with me—I'm gonna' send it ahead!
MUSIC:	BRIDGE
SOUND:	PHONE RINGS…RECEIVER UP.
LANG:	Hello?
CLARA:	(FILTER) Blanche? It's me, Clara.
LANG:	Oh, hello, Clara.
CLARA:	I just called to find out how John likes the trailer you bought.
LANG:	It's parked right in front of the house, but John hasn't seen it yet. He's still at the insurance doctor's office. But I know he'll— (SOUND OF KEY IN LOCK) he's coming in now…I'll call you back, Clara. (HANGS UP. DOOR OPENS & CLOSES) Hello, John. I've got a lovely surprise for you.
PARK:	Later, darling! Come here and let me kiss you first.
LANG:	What?
PARK:	You'll never find me grumpy or irritable again. What's more I want you to take all my bourbon and pour it down the drain!
LANG:	Oh, this is awful.
PARK:	What's awful?
LANG:	The roast caught fire, I burned my finger in the soup, the bathroom door has been stuck all day, and now you come home drunk!

PARK:	What are you talking about? I've never been more sober in my life. And I promised the doctor that I'd never touch another drop of bourbon.
LANG:	Really, John?
PARK:	Yep. He convinced me that losing my temper makes my blood pressure rise, and instead of taking a drink when I lose my temper I'm supposed to eat something.
LANG:	Sounds wonderful. But will it work?
PARK:	Of course. Why, on the way home tonight I ran out of gas and had to push the car for five blocks to a gas station. (CHUCKLES) I didn't find out till later that I had the brake on.
LANG:	You must have been angry.
PARK:	I was furious—but I just calmly chewed on a hotdog.
LANG:	I can hardly believe it.
PARK:	That's nothing. When I pulled up in front of the house just now my brakes didn't hold and I plowed right into a big trailer some idiot parked there.
LANG:	You didn't!
PARK:	I shoved it right over next to a fireplug! It ruined both of my fenders and broke my bumper—but I just sat there eating a banana...Now what's the surprise you have for me, dear?
LANG:	John, that trailer you ran into—
PARK:	Yes?
LANG:	I bought it with your insurance money this morning.
PARK:	Oh, Blanche...Quick—give me a plate of ham and eggs!
MUSIC:	BRIDGE.
HOLBROOK:	(CHUCKLES) In a moment, we'll join the 'happy' Bickersons. Right now, it's time to join our roving reporter, Jay Jackson, for the story of his interview with an actual smoker in Washington, D.C. Okay, Jay Jackson! (SWITCH TO INTERVIEW) RECORDING
JACKSON:	Hello there. This is Jay Jackson. While we've been setting up our microphones here at the corner of Capitol and Louisiana Avenues in the nation's capitol, my assistant has located a volunteer to take the PHILIP MORRIS Nose Test. Are we all set, Frank?

FRANK: All set, Jay. Jay, I'd like you to meet Mr. Howard Smith from West Orange, New Jersey. Mr. Smith is not a PHILIP MORRIS smoker.

JACKSON: Thank you, Frank. How do you do, Mr. Smith.

SMITH: How do you do.

JACKSON: About this test, I'd like to ask you one favor first. For obvious reasons, please do not refer to your present cigarette by its brand name. All right?

SMITH: All right.

JACKSON: All right, fine, Mr. Smith. Now, let me offer you a PHILIP MORRIS cigarette. There we are. Now, do you have one of your own brand handy?

SMITH: Yes I do.

JACKSON: Would you take that out please.

SMITH: Sure.

JACKSON: Now, Mr. Smith, which of the two cigarettes would you like to light first.

SMITH: Well, I'll try the PHILIP MORRIS.

JACKSON: The PHILIP MORRIS first. All right, sir. I'll light it for you—then I want you to take a puff, without inhaling and let the smoke come slowly through your nose. There we are. That's the idea. And that was the PHILIP MORRIS first, right?

SMITH: Right.

JACKSON: Now, sir, let's try exactly the same test with your own brand...

SMITH: All right.

JACKSON: ...which I see is also one of the leading cigarettes. I'll give you a light, take a puff, do not inhale, and let the smoke come slowly through your nose. That's it.

SMITH: The PHILIP MORRIS is much milder.

JACKSON: Well, you said it without my even asking you. You found the PHILIP MORRIS milder...

SMITH: That's right.

JACKSON: ...than your own brand. Well, Mr. Smith, you've confirmed the judgement of thousands of other smokers all over the country—who've also found that PHILIP MORRIS is milder. Thank you very much.

END OF RECORDING

LEAD OUT

FROM COMMERCIAL #2

HOLBROOK: Remember this...the test you just heard is entirely voluntary and no promise of any kind, no payment whatsoever, is made for any statement in the interview. Friends, the PHILIP MORRIS nose test is the only fair test, for it allows you to compare, match, judge PHILIP MORRIS against ANY OTHER CIGARETTE. Yes, try this test—BELIEVE IN YOURSELF—and you too will believe in PHILIP MORRIS, America's FINEST Cigarette!

(PAUSE) And now...The Bickersons...

THEME: (SOFT AND PLAINTIVE).

HOLBROOK: Wild horses couldn't drag the obstinate John on a vacation in a trailer, but Blanche Bickerson is a nag of a different color. So two o'clock in the morning finds the Bickerson automobile moving in the general direction of Yellowstone National Park. (CAR IN...FADE UNDER). This is John Bickerson's first vacation in seven years and his wife Blanche is determined to see that he gets a good rest. They have been driving steadily for nine hours. Listen.

LANG: John.

PARK: Mmmmmmm.

LANG: Don't slump like that.

PARK: I'm not slumping.

LANG: You are too. Your eyes are almost closed and your head keeps lolling on my shoulder.

PARK: Well, I'm sleepy, Blanche. I can't drive anymore.

LANG: You're not driving—I am!

PARK: Oh.

LANG: You haven't touched the wheel for the last eight hours. I've driven all the way since we left that gas station in Bakersfield.

PARK: What were we doing in Bakersfield?

LANG: You and the car got tanked up at the same time. I'm warning you, John Bickerson, I'm not going to stand for your conduct much longer. I'm growing old having to battle with you because of your acts. What do you think I am?

PARK: Old battle-axe.

LANG: What?!

PARK: Put out the lights, Blanche.

LANG: What are you talking about?

PARK: I don't know, I'm not listening. Drive careful, Blanche. Goodnight.

LANG: I wish we'd never started on this trip.

PARK: Ssshhh.

LANG: I won't shush! You've got no right to treat me like a truckdriver. You haven't been one minute's help to me. I don't know where I'm going. I can't understand these dials on the dashboard. I'm telling you now, John, if you fall asleep once more I'll run out of gas.

PARK: You say it, but you won't do it.

LANG: That settles it. (CAR PULLS TO STOP). I'm not going to drive another step!

PARK: Well, pull over to the side. You can't stop in the middle of the highway. You're blocking traffic.

LANG: Oh, all right. (STARTER BUTTONS...MOTOR DOESN'T START...TRIES AGAIN). It won't start.

PARK: Let me see that gas gauge—empty! Why didn't you tell me we were running low?

LANG: I told you I didn't know anything about it.

PARK: Well, there's no use sitting here. There's only one way to get this outfit over to the side of the road and that's by pushing it. (CAR DOOR OPENS). You don't touch a thing till I tell you (FOOTSTEPS ON ROAD). Okay, Blanche!

LANG: (OFF) I can't even budge it, John. You come out and push!

PARK: Wait a minute. Let me try this start—you didn't have the ignition key on. (STARTS CAR...PULLS IT OVER TO SIDE...STOPS) That's that.

LANG: Turn off the headlights, John, and come back here in the trailer...Where did I put that suitcase with my nightgown? John! John! Where is he? What's he doing in that car? (FOOTSTEPS).

PARK: (SNORES LUSTILY...WHINES...SNORES AND WHINES)

LANG: How can that man sleep with his head in the glove compartment?

PARK: (SNORES AND GIGGLES)

LANG: I can't believe it. John!

PARK:	(SNORES AND GIGGLES MERRILY).
LANG:	Oh, stop it! Get out of there!
PARK:	Get out of there, Blanche. Wassamatter? What time is it, Blanche?
LANG:	Come on out of that car and get to sleep in the trailer. Watch your step. (THEY START WALKING BACK)
PARK:	I'm sleepy. I don't wanna open my eyes.
LANG:	Go on—get in. Take your clothes off.
PARK:	Where's the bed?
LANG:	Just pull down the ironing board and hook it to the breadbox.
PARK:	I can't sleep on an ironing board! What kind of a trailer is this?
LANG:	You don't have to sleep on the ironing board. That just makes the slats. (SHE HOOKS IT) Now you just fold the stove underneath and slide the seat pads on top. There. Isn't that clever?
PARK:	Wonderful. Goodnight.
LANG:	The other bed hooks on the other side. (SHE HOOKS IT) See how simple it is?
PARK:	I hate it.
LANG:	Oh, you're never satisfied with anything. This trailer's a darn sight better than our apartment if you ask me.
PARK:	Mmmmmm.
LANG:	It's got every modern convenience. There's more closet space than we have, there's a lovely metal sink, and the bathroom is out of this world.
PARK:	That's what I was afraid of. Blow out the candle, Blanche.
LANG:	It's not a candle. It's an electric bulb shaped like a candle.
PARK:	Well, turn it off and go to sleep. I've never been so tired in all my life.
LANG:	Well, if it won't trouble you too much I'd like to get my clothes off. Would you mind unzipping my back?
PARK:	Back up. (ZIP RIP)
LANG:	Thanks.
PARK:	Here's the zipper.
LANG:	John Bickerson!

PARK: Oh, I couldn't help it. The darn thing came off in my hand. Why don't they sew it on tight?

LANG: I'm going to take it back to Madame Selma's and get a refund. Then I'm going out to buy some real clothes.

PARK: You've got plenty of clothes.

LANG: I have not.

PARK: You have too. You spend a fortune on clothes.

LANG: How can you say that! All I own is this dress and that red dinner gown. And I got that gown for a ridiculous figure.

PARK: Well, you were fatter then.

LANG: I'm talking about the price! Don't you go babbling about me spending money for clothes. Is it a crime if I need a new dress?

PARK: You always need a new dress. When I married you, you didn't have a rag on your back—now you're covered with 'em. That's not what I mean!

LANG: It's true, though. All I've got is rags. And you scream your head off if I buy one dress a year. In another two months, I'll have absolutely nothing to wear around the house. Then what'll I do?

PARK: Pull down the shades.

LANG: Believe me, Gloria Gooseby got the right kind of a husband. That Leo gives her everything and he never squawks!

PARK: Ahhhhh!

LANG: Leo covers her with diamonds and bundles her in furs. Leo bought her a blue mink coat last month, and the month before that Leo gave her a pearl necklace. I saw her last week and what do you think she's got wrapped around her little finger?

PARK: Leo.

LANG: No, she hasn't. She's got a ring with a diamond in it as big as my head.

PARK: Maybe it's as big, but I'll bet it's not as thick.

LANG: You be careful how you talk to me, John!

PARK: Well, you're always riling me up! I didn't start anything—you did! You wanna do nothing but fight. fight, fight!

LANG: Keep quiet—you'll wake the neighbors.

PARK: What neighbors? We're in a trailer a million miles from everybody!

LANG: I wish I was home.

PARK: So do I. Goodnight.

LANG: Oh, John—can't we even enjoy ourselves for one week? I didn't mean to start anything.

PARK: Well, go to bed. I'm so tired I don't know what I'm doing.

LANG: All right. Hand me my cold cream from the overnight bag, will you please, John? It's right under your bed.

PARK: (FUMBLES THRU BAG) How do you jam all this stuff into one small bag? Hair nets, bobbie pins, slippers, stockings, bathrobe. Here's your cold cream.

LANG: Thanks, dear.

PARK: What's this? Since when do they put fur on 'em?

LANG: All earmuffs have fur on them.

PARK: Oh, they're earmuffs. Are you ready for bed now?

LANG: Yes, dear.

PARK: Goodnight.

LANG: Let's talk.

PARK: Blanche, I don't feel like talking. I wanna sleep.

LANG: I don't understand you. I swear I don't. You never want to talk. Not to me, anyway. I mean a real conversation, John.

PARK: Mmmm.

LANG: Do you know you haven't actually spoken to me for three months.

PARK: Mmmm.

LANG: Why is that, John?

PARK: I didn't want to interrupt you.

LANG: See? Then you say I start everything. Can't you say something nice to me just once in your life? Must you always dig at me?

PARK: Blanche, it's three o'clock in the morning.

LANG: I don't care. I try to be sweet to you and you won't even be civil.

PARK: Oh, dear.

LANG: I'll bet there isn't another woman alive who has to humiliate herself the way I do to get a kind word from her husband. Why did you marry me if you can't stand the sight of me?

PARK: I can stand the sight of you.

LANG:	But you don't love me.
PARK:	Yes, I do.
LANG:	You don't, you don't, you don't.
PARK:	I tell you I do!
LANG:	Then why don't you say it!
PARK:	I've said it until I'm blue in the face! I've made records in seven different languages! I've got your face embroidered on my shorts! I even offered to stamp out "John Loves Blanche" with a hot branding iron, didn't I? You wouldn't let me do it, would you?
LANG:	No.
PARK:	Why not?
LANG:	Because it was burning my hip!
PARK:	Well, if you can't stand a little pain don't keep asking for proof of my love. I'm gonna tell you for the last time, Blanche—no man ever felt about a woman the way I feel about you!
LANG:	Honest?
PARK:	Honest!
LANG:	Do you really despise me?
PARK:	You know I do.
LANG:	What!
PARK:	I mean no! Please don't start that all over again, Blanche.
LANG:	Well, I can't help feeling—what was that?
PARK:	What was what?
LANG:	Outside the trailer. I thought I heard somebody prowling around. Get up and look, John.
PARK:	Oh, there's nobody there.
LANG:	You left the keys in the car. Why don't you get up and look?
PARK:	There's nothing to look for.
LANG:	That proves you don't love me. You once told me you'd face death for me, didn't you?
PARK:	Yes.
LANG:	Then why don't you go see who it is?
PARK:	How do I know he's dead?

LANG:	John, if anybody breaks in here will you save me?
PARK:	Yes, I'll save you.
LANG:	Why?
PARK:	Oh, what's the matter with you, Blanche? Why don't you just calm down and go to sleep?
LANG:	I can't sleep. I'm worried.
PARK:	I tell you there's nobody outside.
LANG:	It's not that. I've got something to tell you.
PARK:	Well, tell me.
LANG:	If you give me a kiss I'll tell you.
PARK:	Tell me now and I'll kiss you later.
LANG:	You might not feel like kissing me later.
PARK:	I don't feel like kissing you now. Not after the way you upset me. What have you done?
LANG:	You remember when we stopped for gas in Las Vegas?
PARK:	I remember.
LANG:	Well, I went into the washroom to powder my nose and they had a slot machine built into the mirror.
PARK:	You went for it, huh? How many nickels did you lose?
LANG:	It was a dollar machine.
PARK:	Blanche! You didn't lose a dollar!
LANG:	I lost forty-seven dollars.
PARK:	Forty-seven dollars! You squandered my life savings on a one-armed bandit!
LANG:	I was only trying to make enough to pay for the—
PARK:	How can you throw away my money like that! I work like a slave to hold on to a few pennies! I deny myself everything! I've been sewing collars on your old girdles and wearing 'em for turtle-neck sweaters! I don't even own a pair of pants, I just wear a long coat and walk to work on my knees! And she gambles away forty-seven dollars! I never gambled in my life.
LANG:	Last week you bought a raffle-ticket for a quarter.
PARK:	What raffle! It was a pawn-ticket—I hocked my teeth! Blanche, I take an oath—

LANG:	John! Quick—there's somebody unhitching the car!
PARK:	Don't try to change the subject! We're gonna have a showdown if it's—
LANG:	John! (CAR STARTS UP AND PULLS AWAY) Look out the window!
PARK:	What are you talking about? Where? (GETS OUT OF BED) What happened to the car, Blanche? It's gone!
LANG:	I told you there was a prowler! You wouldn't listen!
PARK:	Ohhhhh! How do we get the police? That crook made off with my car!
LANG:	Well, you don't have to get hysterical, John! He can't get away with it.
PARK:	Why not?
LANG:	Because I copied down his license number.
PARK:	Oh, what's the use! Goodnight, Blanche.
LANG:	Goodnight, John.
MUSIC:	BICKERSON PLAYOFF
	(APPLAUSE)
HOLBROOK:	Frances Langford and Lew Parker are standing by for a curtain call. In the meantime, for America's FINEST Cigarette, here's another call well-worth remembering…
JOHNNY:	CALL…FOR…PHILIP MORRIS!
MUSIC:	"ON THE TRAIL" THEME
HOLBROOK:	Remember: PHILIP MORRIS is definitely less irritating, definitely milder than any other leading brand. Remember: NO CIGARETTE HANGOVER means MORE SMOKING PLEASURE—so…
JOHNNY:	CALL…FOR…PHILIP…MORRIS!
HOLBROOK:	And now, here are John and Blanche Bickerson as Frances Langford and Lew Parker.
LANG:	Oh, Lew—I wanted to remind you that you and your wife are expected at the Hawaiian Luau I'm giving Sunday night.
PARK:	I haven't forgotten, Frances. As a matter of fact, I'm gonna bring along my own personal recipe for Hawaiian Punch.
LANG:	Wonderful. How do you make it, Lew?
PARK:	Oh, you just get a large galvanized iron tub and pour in a bottle of rum, a bottle of brandy, gin, dubbonet, scotch and rye and a slice of pineapple. Then mix it all together—and this is the important part—you must drink it outdoors.

LANG:	Why can't you drink it indoors?
PARK:	Because the last time I served it somebody hiccuped and set fire to the drapes.
LANG:	Goodnight, Lew.
PARK:	Goodnight, Frances. Goodnight, everybody.
HOLBROOK:	Be sure to listen next Tuesday night when PHILIP MORRIS again will present The Bickersons. And don't miss the PHILIP MORRIS Playhouse this coming Thursday night over this same station when PHILIP MORRIS will present_____ starring in_____. That's Thursday night for the PHILIP MORRIS Playhouse, over CBS. In the meantime…don't forget to…
JOHNNY:	CALL…FOR…PHILIP…MORRIS!
MUSIC:	UP
	(APPLAUSE)
HOLBROOK:	The Bickersons came to you from Hollywood, California. John Holbrook speaking.
	THIS IS THE CBS…RADIO…NETWORK!

TV BIT (FIREMAN JOHN)

(REVISED)

CONTE: And now, ladies and gentlemen, here are Frances Langford and Lew Parker as John and Blanche Bickerson in "The Honeymoon is Over"!

THEME: SOFT AND PLAINTIVE

CONTE: Blanche Bickerson has retired. In the absence of husband John she is finally managing to get some much needed sleep. Heaven knows she's earned it after eight years of John's pseudo-insomnia, which manifests itself in the most ear shattering snores ever produced by man or beast. Tonight you will sleep well, dear Blanche—

FADE IN BICKERSON BEDROOM.

SOUND: TELEPHONE RINGS

—oh-oh! I should have bitten my tongue!

(The phone continues to ring three or four times. Blanche pulls herself out of her sleep, goes to the phone, lifts receiver)

BLANCHE: Hello.

CLARA: (VOICE FILTER) Blanche? It's me, Clara. Did I wake you up?

BLANCHE: Yes. What's the matter with you, Clara? Why are you calling me at four o'clock in the morning?

CLARA: Well, I had to get up anyway. I don't mind it.

BLANCHE: Well, I mind it. I've been sick all day. I'd like to sleep.

CLARA: Uh-huh. Well, I was just giving little George his formula and I thought I'd call. He's on a four o'clock feeding now, you know.

BLANCHE: No, I didn't know.

CLARA: He gets nine feedings a night. I just put his chops on the stove.

BLANCHE: Chops! For a three-month-old child?

CLARA: Oh, I puree them. Barney eats most of it anyway. Is John sleeping?

BLANCHE: No—he's at work.

CLARA: This time of the morning? I thought he didn't leave until seven.

BLANCHE: He still leaves at seven. But he took on an extra job.

CLARA: How does he get all those jobs, Blanche? What's he doing now?

BLANCHE: He's hooked up with an engine company—or ladders, or something—I don't know. He just started today.

CLARA: Can he get Barney in there?

BLANCHE: No, he can't get Barney in there. And Clara, I wish you—oh, I think I hear him coming now. I'll talk to you tomorrow.

CLARA: Huh?

BLANCHE: Goodbye.

(She hangs up and gets back in bed. John enters. HE IS DRESSED IN A FIREMAN'S SLICKER, RUBBER BOOTS AND METAL HAT AND CARRIES A REGULAR FIREMAN'S AXE. Without a word he places his axe near his bed, notices his pillow is missing, trudges to the bathroom. In a moment he returns carrying the cat and his pillow. He throws the pillow on his bed, picks up his axe and walks towards the kitchen)

BLANCHE: John! What are you going to do?

(He throws the cat in the kitchen, returns and replaces his axe. Then he strips the pillow case off the pillow, tosses it away and glares at Blanche)

BLANCHE: Don't be angry with Nature Boy, John. It's my fault.

JOHN: Mmm.

BLANCHE: I gave him your pillow because he wasn't feeling good when he came in.

JOHN: He was feeling fine when he was out!

BLANCHE: What do you mean?

JOHN: Two hours ago I had to climb up a telephone pole and rescue the beast!

BLANCHE: What was the frightened little thing doing on top of a telephone pole?

JOHN: Frightened little thing? He chased a St. Bernard up it! Don't talk to me, Blanche.

(He takes off his rubber boots and discloses bare feet)

BLANCHE: What have I done? Why are you mad at me, John?

JOHN: I don't wanna talk. Go to sleep.

TV Bit (Fireman John) • 171

(He takes off his raincoat and hangs it on a hall-tree. Underneath he is wearing regulation fireman's pants held up by brilliant red suspenders. He removes his pants and reveals his pajamas. He gets in bed, places his hat beneath it)

JOHN: Put out the lights.

BLANCHE: Put out the lights? Is that what they taught you at the firehouse? Can't I receive some other greeting?

JOHN: I wish I'd receive mine.

BLANCHE: No kiss—no hug. You know I've been sick as a dog all day.

JOHN: Mmm.

BLANCHE: You might at least ask me how I feel.

JOHN: I'll ask you in the morning.

BLANCHE: Why don't you ask me now?

JOHN: All right—how do you feel?

BLANCHE: None of your business!

JOHN: Blanche, what do you want from me? I have to get up in two hours and go to my regular job. I spent the whole night at the firehouse working my axe off! Why don't you let me get some rest?

BLANCHE: Did I tell you to take a job as a fireman? What did you do it for if it makes you so mad?

JOHN: I only took the job because I thought I could get some sleep.

BLANCHE: Well, why didn't you sleep?

JOHN: Because we had eleven fires in four hours!

BLANCHE: Who told you to go to all of them? Must you be such a hero?

JOHN: What do you mean hero? The whole engine company has to go.

BLANCHE: How did you know they weren't false alarms?

JOHN: You don't know until you get there!

BLANCHE: Well, that's pretty silly. Why would you go there if it's a false alarm?

JOHN: Blanche, please leave me alone. My hands ache from hanging on the truck, my back aches from dragging the hose and my legs ache from sliding down the pole!

BLANCHE: Sliding down a pole? What do you land on?

JOHN: That aches too. And I'll tell you right now I'm not going back there! I'm quitting!

BLANCHE: Go ahead and quit—see if I care! You're the one who said you needed the extra money.

JOHN: I'd rather starve.

BLANCHE: Well, I wouldn't. And since you brought up the subject of money—

JOHN: *I* brought up the subject!

BLANCHE: Yes. I'd like you to let me have an extra twenty dollars this week.

JOHN: I can't let you have it this week.

BLANCHE: That's what you said last week.

JOHN: Well, I kept my promise, didn't I? Put out the lights.

BLANCHE: I will not. I'm tired of slaving for you and getting no appreciation. I spend half my life cooking your meals and what do I get out of it? Nothing.

JOHN: You're lucky—I get indigestion.

BLANCHE: That's right—now complain about my cooking.

JOHN: I'm not complaining. You're the best cook in the world.

BLANCHE: That's not true. I can't even boil water.

JOHN: I know it.

BLANCHE: Then why do you keep telling everybody you married me because I was a wonderful cook?

JOHN: I have to give 'em some excuse.

BLANCHE: Oh, you'll pay for that John Bickerson.

JOHN: I'm sorry. I'm sorry, I'm sorry, I'm sorry!

BLANCHE: It's easy to say you're sorry now.

JOHN: No it isn't.

BLANCHE: Well, you're not going to get away with it. I don't care where you get the money—but I'm going to have some new clothes. I'm sick of walking around looking like an old frump.

JOHN: Mmm.

BLANCHE: It's true, isn't it?

JOHN: What's true?

BLANCHE: I look like an old frump.

JOHN: I wouldn't say that.

BLANCHE: Why not, John?

JOHN: I'll only be awake for the rest of the night.

BLANCHE: Wherever I go people point at me and sneer. They say, "There goes Bickerson's wife—look how she's dressed!"

JOHN: For heaven's sake—I'm Bickerson and look how I'm dressed!

BLANCHE: I don't care. I'm entitled to something out of this marriage. You never take me anywhere. You never buy me anything.

JOHN: What are you talking about? I take you everywhere and it isn't two weeks ago that I bought you a Fifth of perfume.

BLANCHE: It was horrible. It burned a hole in my dress.

JOHN: Well, you're not supposed to use more than a jigger behind each ear! There was nothing wrong with that perfume—it tasted fine.

BLANCHE: Tasted fine! Now I'm beginning to understand why you kissed me when I wore it.

JOHN: That had nothing to do with it.

BLANCHE: Not much! I never saw a man so cold and unaffectionate.

JOHN: Don't you talk about affection. The only time you're affectionate is when you want money!

BLANCHE: Well, isn't that often enough?

JOHN: You can say that again. Put out the lights and let me get some sleep, will you, Blanche?

BLANCHE: No I won't. The minute you go to sleep you'll start that awful snoring. Why don't you go back to the firehouse?

JOHN: Never snore.

BLANCHE: You snore all the time. Every night of your life. So what do you do tonight?

(He snores and whines. She stares at him. He snores and whines again. As he continues to snore she picks up the alarm clock and sets the alarm off. He leaps out of bed, puts on his hat, and slides down the hall-tree)

JOHN: Women and children first!

(He grabs his axe and starts chopping up a carton near his bed)

BLANCHE: John! What are you doing!

JOHN: What happened?

BLANCHE: Get back in bed, you crazy man. You've probably ruined that package.

JOHN: What package? What's in it?

BLANCHE: I don't know. It came from Kentucky today.

JOHN: (Grabbing it up)

The Bottle of the Month Club! This is my yearly dividend! Why didn't you tell me, Blanche.

BLANCHE: Well, don't get hysterical,

(As he starts for the kitchen)

Where are you going with it?

JOHN: Gotta put it in a safe place.

(He enters the kitchen. There is a body slam and glass crash)

JOHN: Owww! I'll kill that cat! Where's the light?...Ohh! My bourbon!

BLANCHE: Did it break?

JOHN: My pajamas are all wet. I hope it's blood.

BLANCHE: Get off your knees and stop licking the floor!

(He returns with his pajama coat soaked. He goes to his dresser and wrings it out in a glass, and then drinks it. He gets back in bed)

JOHN: Put out the lights.

BLANCHE: Is there any glass on the kitchen floor?

JOHN: I don't know and I don't care. All I wanna do is sleep, Blanche.

BLANCHE: I don't see how you can sleep anyway. Aren't you thinking about tomorrow?

JOHN: I'm thinking.

BLANCHE: I suppose you've forgotten what tomorrow is.

JOHN: Haven't forgotten.

BLANCHE: Well, what is it?

JOHN: It's our wedding anniversary.

BLANCHE: No it isn't. It's rent day.

JOHN: Oh. Well, I knew it was a sad occasion of some kind.

BLANCHE: Now what was that dirty dig for?

JOHN: No dirty dig. Just let me sleep.

BLANCHE: I can just hear you saying that to Gloria Gooseby.

JOHN: Now don't start with Gloria Gooseby!

BLANCHE: You wouldn't think it was a sad occasion if you married her!

JOHN: I didn't marry her and it's the saddest occasion of my life! I mean, I hate the sight of Gloria Gooseby and I wouldn't go near her for a million dollars!

BLANCHE: I swear I don't know what you see in that woman.

JOHN: I don't see anything in her.

BLANCHE: She may have a pretty face and a nice figure—but I've got brains, and after all it's the little things that count.

JOHN: Go to sleep.

BLANCHE: Some day you'll appreciate me, John Bickerson. But it'll be too late. I won't be around to pester you much longer.

JOHN: What's the matter, Blanche?

BLANCHE: Nothing.

JOHN: What's the matter with you? Are you sick again?

BLANCHE: So sick I could die. I told you this morning but you never pay any attention. I was even too sick to see the doctor.

JOHN: What hurts you?

BLANCHE: I think it's my liver. And I know there's no cure for it.

JOHN: Yes there is. Rub it with chicken fat.

BLANCHE: What kind of an insane remedy is that?

JOHN: Best thing in the world for liver. Chicken fat. You want me to fix it?

BLANCHE: You leave me alone. You'll treat me for liver trouble and I'll probably die of indigestion.

JOHN: Listen, if I treat you for liver trouble you'll die of liver trouble! Now do you want me to help you or not?

BLANCHE: No!

JOHN: Goodnight.

BLANCHE: Get up and bring me the thermometer.

(He struggles out of bed, looks for his slipper)

JOHN: Where's my slipper?

BLANCHE: You took it to work with you. Hurry up and bring the thermometer—I'm burning up.

(He takes his slipper out of his boot, puts it on and goes to the kitchen)

JOHN'S VOICE (O.S.): Where's the thermometer? I can't find it.

BLANCHE: It's on the window sill—right next to the garbage can.

JOHN: (Enters with small covered can)

Is this the garbage can?

BLANCHE: Sure it is.

JOHN: I've been taking it to work every day—I thought it was my lunch pail! No wonder nobody ever wants to swap sandwiches with me.

BLANCHE: Well, where's the thermometer?

JOHN: I couldn't find it.

BLANCHE: (Getting out of bed)

Oh, you can't find anything.

(She goes to the kitchen and he sits on the pail. Blanche re-enters with the thermometer)

BLANCHE: Here's the thermometer.

(He takes it, puts it in his mouth and takes his pulse. He removes the thermometer after a few seconds, looks at it)

JOHN: Oh, I'm a sick man. Gotta get some sleep. Goodnight.

(He goes back to bed)

BLANCHE: (Getting in bed)

That's the attention you give me. Always thinking of yourself.

JOHN: I'm sick, I tell you.

BLANCHE: Then we're both sick. Maybe that's why we fight so much. What are we going to do, John? Maybe we ought to go away on a vacation?

JOHN: Fine.

BLANCHE: How would you like to go to Atlantic City?

JOHN: Okay. Where will you go?

BLANCHE: See! You're starting again.

TV Bit (Fireman John) • 177

JOHN: I'm not starting, Blanche. I'm so sleepy I don't know what I'm saying.

BLANCHE: You must hate me terribly!

JOHN: Not terribly!

BLANCHE: You don't love me.

JOHN: Yes I do.

BLANCHE: You don't, you don't, you don't.

JOHN: I tell you I do, Blanche.

BLANCHE: Do you love me only?

JOHN: Yes.

BLANCHE: When I'm away from you?

JOHN: Yes.

BLANCHE: Well, say it.

JOHN: I love you only when you're away from me. Put out the lights.

BLANCHE: John, why are you so mean to me? Am I so hard to please?

JOHN: I don't know—I never tried to please you.

BLANCHE: How well I know it! That's why you don't want to take me away on a vacation.

JOHN: Blanche, how can I take you on a vacation? If I take two weeks off from work we're wiped out.

BLANCHE: Barney never works and he takes Clara on vacation.

JOHN: If that bum Barney doesn't work where does he get the dough?

BLANCHE: Accident insurance. He's collected a fortune on accident insurance.

JOHN: Accident insurance?

BLANCHE: Yes. Every time Clara has a baby he jumps off the roof.

JOHN: What!

BLANCHE: He doesn't hurt himself too bad—just enough to collect the insurance. You haven't got any, have you, John?

JOHN: No. And I don't wanna talk about it—I wanna sleep.

BLANCHE: But suppose something happens to you? What if you have an accident and you can't work?

JOHN: Then we'll starve.

BLANCHE: We're starving now.

JOHN: Too bad.

BLANCHE: It's easy for you to talk like that—but if anything happened I'd be left helpless and destitute. Why don't you get some accident insurance, John?

JOHN: I'll get some next week.

BLANCHE: You say it but you won't do it. Do it now.

JOHN: What?

BLANCHE: Go on—get up and get some accident insurance!

JOHN: Blanche, are you out of your mind! It's almost three o'clock in the morning!

BLANCHE: Well, people have accidents all hours of the night.

JOHN: I'm not gonna have any accidents tonight!

BLANCHE: How do you know?

JOHN: Blanche, why don't you let me sleep?

BLANCHE: Well, just promise you'll get some accident insurance.

JOHN: Why?

BLANCHE: Because it's a wonderful protection. Clara told me two weeks ago a man broke his hip and he got five hundred dollars. Last week Barney fractured his skull and got a thousand dollars.

JOHN: What about it?

BLANCHE: Next week you may be the lucky one!

JOHN: Goodnight, Blanche.

BLANCHE: Goodnight, John.

CURTAIN

COFFEE RICH COMMERCIALS
Rich Advertising Co.

Commercial #3

The Bickersons   Feature: Cooking   Locale: Camping

SOUND:	Bird Calls…Anything to establish outdoors.
JOHN:	(OFF…CALLING) Holy smoke— I'm lost in the brush! Blanche—where are you! Blanche!
BLANCHE:	I'm right here by the tent. Is that you, John?
JOHN:	(FADING IN) Who did you expect in the middle of this wilderness—Richard Burton? Boy, I'm exhausted! Any coffee?
BLANCHE:	Here—I kept it nice and hot. And here's the Coffee Rich—pour in all you want. I've got two extra cartons.
JOHN:	How do you keep the stuff so fresh?
BLANCHE:	In the cooler. Coffee Rich stays fresh for three weeks. Did you catch any fish?
JOHN:	Plenty. Get them out of the creel while I stoke up the campfire.
BLANCHE:	John! What are these tiny things—they look like sardines!
JOHN:	Yeah—well, the trout are running kind of small this year.
BLANCHE:	Uh-huh. What do you want me to do with this sardine can?
JOHN:	Don't be snide! That's to hold my dry files! Just cook up those beautiful trout with a couple of steaks and some fried potatoes and we'll have plenty to eat.
BLANCHE:	I knew you wouldn't catch anything so I made this Beef Stroganoff. Look.
JOHN:	Beef Stroganoff over a campfire? Are you kidding?
BLANCHE:	It's easy. The meat cooked in no time and I used Coffee Rich as a base for the sauce.
JOHN:	What's with this Coffee Rich? You've been putting it on the cereal, on the fruit, in the eggs—
BLANCHE:	That's because it improves everything I cook. Don't you like it?

JOHN:	Sure. But it's a good thing we're going home tomorrow. With all these creamy foods I'll put on four pounds!
BLANCHE:	No you won't. Coffee Rich has fewer calories per ounce than cream and it costs less. It's a non-dairy product.
JOHN:	Yeah.
BLANCHE:	Taste this Beef Stroganoff. Go on—notice how Coffee Rich brings out the flavor in the sauce.
JOHN:	Mmm...(TASTES)...Beef Stroganoff.
BLANCHE:	How is it?
JOHN:	Blanche—if you don't mind I'll just eat the sauce!
BLANCHE:	I knew you'd start picking on my—
JOHN:	Okay, okay! I'll eat it—I'll eat it!
ANNCR:	You've just heard that ever-lovin' couple, "The Bickersons," starring Don Ameche, Frances Langford and Coffee Rich, the leading liquid non-dairy creamer. Why not let Coffee Rich star in your home with its delicious taste and low cost? Find it in your grocer's freezer in the blue and white carton.

SUPERMARKET SPOT

BLANCHE:	(EXCITEDLY) Look, John. They have mynah bird feed on sale at half price.
JOHN:	We don't have a mynah bird, Blanche.
BLANCHE:	Every time I see a really good special, there's a catch. Oh, look at those darling old fashioned lamp chimneys.
JOHN:	Are you trying to open your own supermarket? We don't have any old fashioned lamps.
BLANCHE:	(TEARFULLY) John, you never buy me anything.
JOHN:	We haven't bought the Coffee Rich we came in for and you've got two shopping carts full already.
BLANCHE:	What's wrong with that?
JOHN:	I can't push two carts.
BLANCHE:	Then try pulling one. Oh, here's the freezer case with the Coffee Rich. I'll take four.
JOHN:	Where do you plan to put them?

BLANCHE: Where I always do. On your cereal of course, and on your fruit and in your coffee. Coffee Rich makes everything taste better.

JOHN: Then fix me a bowl and I'll eat it right here. There's no room on the carts.

BLANCHE: I can't. You know the Coffee Rich comes frozen. That's why you can keep extras on hand in the freezer. Even after it's thawed it stays fresh three weeks in the refrigerator.

JOHN: Then that's where I should be. You wear me out.

BLANCHE: Just let me get the Coffee Rich aboard and we'll go. There's one carton.

JOHN: If we eat all this we'll turn into blimps.

BLANCHE: Just eat the Coffee Rich, it's low in calories. There's a second carton.

JOHN: (ALARMEDLY) Look out, Blanche, it won't work.

BLANCHE: And here goes the last carton.

(SOUND OF ALL KINDS OF PACKAGES CRASHING TO FLOOR)

JOHN: And there goes two hours of shopping. At least the Coffee Rich didn't break. It's frozen.

ANNCR: Now you know where to buy Coffee Rich. In your grocer's freezer case.

DUCK SHOOTING SPOT

SOUND: (SWAMP NOISES. DUCK QUACKING)

JOHN: Blanche, pour me a cup of coffee while we're waiting.

BLANCHE: (POURS) Here you are, dear.

JOHN: Boy, that's good. Ever since we got Coffee Rich even your coffee tastes great!

BLANCHE: And how about your morning cereal and fruit. And my soups and sauces.

JOHN: They're all good. Coffee Rich has made a new woman out of you. Now look, Blanche, here's what we do. When the ducks fly over, I'll take my shot. If I get one, let go of the dog.

BLANCHE: The dog. Oh, my heavens, I left him back at the lodge, John.

JOHN: You what? For Pete's sake. Oh well, we could probably stay out here for three weeks and wouldn't see a duck anyway.

BLANCHE:	Three weeks. That's exactly how long Coffee Rich stays fresh and flavorful in the refrigerator. Keeps frozen for months. And Coffee Rich tastes better than cream and costs less too. Also has less calories.
JOHN:	I know all that, Blanche. (PAUSE) Listen! Do you hear something?
SOUND:	(FLOCK OF DUCKS GRADUALLY GETTING CLOSER)
SOUND:	(FIRING OF SHOTGUN)
JOHN:	I got one, Blanche! Look at him fall.
BLANCHE:	He's falling in the middle of the pond.
JOHN:	Start swimming, Blanche. And don't bite down on the duck.
ANNCR:	Retrieve the old-fashioned flavor of good coffee with Coffee Rich, the new non-dairy liquid creamer that tastes better than cream at less cost. And if hunting for an exciting new flavor in cereals, over fruits, in soups and sauces, Coffee Rich again. Look for the blue and white carton in your grocer's frozen food section.

SKIING SPOT

JOHN:	Blanche, Blanche, get me out of this snowdrift!
BLANCHE:	Why don't you stand up?
JOHN:	If I could stand up I wouldn't be here.
BLANCHE:	Here comes help—a St. Bernard.
JOHN:	Oh, boy! Has he got a cask under his neck?
BLANCHE:	He's got a carton of Coffee Rich.
JOHN:	(GROANING) That's all I need in a snowdrift. A frozen carton of Coffee Rich. At least he could have brought me a cup of coffee too.
BLANCHE:	Wouldn't that have been nice of him? Coffee Rich does so much for a cup of coffee. It smooths away the bitterness and brings out all the hearty coffee flavor. And when you think that it costs less than cow's cream and has fewer calories, it's almost too much!
JOHN:	It is too much. I'm freezing to death in a snowbank and you're doing a Coffee Rich commercial.
BLANCHE:	I'll ski down for help, John. You stay here.
JOHN:	Did you think I'd be going to Acapulco?
BLANCHE:	We'll bring you back some nice hot cereal. Coffee Rich brings out the taste of cereal. Adds richness and flavor, just as it does for fruit. The St. Bernard will keep you company while I'm gone. (SOUND OF VOICE FADING AWAY) Good bye-ye-ye, John.

JOHN:	Come here, Rover. Lie down. That's right. Snuggle close. You are warm. (SOUND OF CONTENTED YAWN AND SIGH) H-m-m. Good night, Blanche.
ANNCR:	That was Don Ameche and Frances Langford as "The Bickersons" for Coffee Rich, the all-season, all-around creamer. It's the fastest growing creamer in the country. Frozen, liquid, merely thaw to use. Find it in your grocer's frozen food case.

NATURE BOY SPOT (FEATURE: TASTE)

SOUND:	HAMMERING
BLANCHE:	John? John—what are you doing to my refrigerator?
JOHN:	I'm putting a padlock on it—that's what!
BLANCHE:	You stop that!
JOHN:	I will not! Somebody's been getting at my Coffee Rich.
BLANCHE:	Nobody's been getting at it. I've been feeding it to Nature Boy.
JOHN:	Who's Nature Boy?
BLANCHE:	Our cat, silly. It puts a shine on his coat.
JOHN:	Shine on his coat, huh? How would he like a kick in his pants? You stop giving my Coffee Rich to that monster!
BLANCHE:	Oh, I've got plenty of cartons in the freezer. I give it to Nature Boy because it's the leading non-dairy creamer and it keeps him sleek and slender. You don't like a fat cat, do you?
JOHN:	I hate that monster!
BLANCHE:	You two would get along a lot better if you'd just try to be more friendly with him. Why don't you get him something to play with?
JOHN:	I'll bring him a dog in the morning! Look out—here he comes! (MENACING CAT NOISES…TIGER ROARING) Quick, Blanche—the whip—the chair—the pistol! He's coming at me!
BLANCHE:	Here Nature Boy—here, sweetie…There you are!
SOUND:	CAT MEOWS SOFTLY AND STARTS TO PURR.
BLANCHE:	Okay, John—you can get down off that ladder now.
JOHN:	What did you do to him—he's like a kitten.
BLANCHE:	I just gave him a saucer of Coffee Rich. He knows it tastes better than cream and it changes his disposition.
JOHN:	Sure does.

BLANCHE: That's because it puts more flavor into anything you pour on it. Cereals, fruits, coffee, anything. Maybe in time you'll change your disposition.

JOHN: Now, wait a minute—

BLANCHE: Coffee Rich costs less, too, and it's got fewer calories per ounce than cream. Look at Nature Boy lap it up!

JOHN: I'm still gonna put a padlock on the refrigerator!

SOUND: HAMMERING. FADES UNDER—

ANNCR: That was Don Ameche and Frances Langford in "The Bickersons," sponsored by Coffee Rich. No matter what, those cats keep their cool. Keep yours. Discover new liquid non-dairy Coffee Rich at your grocer's freezer. It comes in the blue and white carton.

BED SPOT (THEME: KEEPING QUALITIES)

JOHN: (SNORES AND WHINES...SNORES AND GIGGLES)

BLANCHE: John! John Bickerson!

JOHN: Mmmm? Wassamatter, Blanche—wassamater.

BLANCHE: Turn over on your side—go on!

JOHN: Okay—OWWWWW! Who put this block of ice in my bed!

BLANCHE: It's not a block of ice. It's a frozen carton of Coffee Rich. Lay on it.

JOHN: Why should I lay on frozen Coffee Rich at four o'clock in the morning?

BLANCHE: Because I want it to thaw out.

JOHN: This is insane!

BLANCHE: Well, I know you love it on your cornflakes, and I forgot to take it out of the freezer in time for your breakfast.

JOHN: Why didn't you sprinkle the cornflakes in here too, then I wouldn't have to get up at all.

BLANCHE: Don't be testy, John. You know Coffee Rich is your favorite non-dairy liquid creamer, and you always scream when I don't have it.

JOHN: Okay. Put out the lights.

BLANCHE: You're lucky you have a wife who understands what Coffee Rich means to you and doesn't get jealous. You like its rich taste better than cream, right?

JOHN: Right. Now, just put—

BLANCHE: You like the way it tastes on cereals, and freshens the flavor of fruits, right?

JOHN: Blanche—

BLANCHE: You like the way you can really pour Coffee Rich on because it has fewer calories per ounce than cream, right?

JOHN: The lights, Blanche—put out the lights!

BLANCHE: You like the way it doesn't spoil in hot weather like this, stays fresh three weeks in the refrigerator, so there's no waste.

JOHN: Oh, dear.

BLANCHE: And you love its new low cost. Now roll over on it and keep it warm.

JOHN: What am I—a mother cow!

BLANCHE: Coffee Rich doesn't need a cow, John. It's the leading liquid non-dairy creamer.

JOHN: Holy mackerel—I married a radio announcer!

ANNCR: Two people who are never are cowed are John and Blanche, "The Bickersons." Played by Don Ameche and Frances Langford. Walk into your grocer's and demand liquid, non-dairy Coffee Rich. You'll find it in his freezer in the blue and white carton.

GM COMMCERCIAL

ANNCR: And now—Don Ameche and Frances Langford as "The Bickersons."

JOHN: (GIRDING FOR BATTLE) I knew it! The new car's gone again! OK, Blanche, which one of your relatives borrowed it this time?

BLANCHE: (SPOILING FOR THE FRAY) My mother!

JOHN: I see! Lady MacBeth rides again!

BLANCHE: It's your own fault, John! When you got that new car with General Motors Four-Season Climate Control, you had to hold a press conference! Kept bragging it up about how much fresher you feel at the wheel with conditioned air…no problems with pollen or excess humidity. Temperature's always just right—every day of the year. Clothes clean and neat. Quiet.

JOHN: For years she avoids me like a plague!…Now I get a car with GM Harrison Climate Control and suddenly I'm "Mister Wonderful!" When'll the Juggernaut be back?

BLANCHE: If you mean "mother," she's returning day after tomorrow.

JOHN: I guess now the only time I can depend on having the car to myself is Halloween.

BLANCHE: Halloween?

JOHN: That's the night she rides her broomstick!

ANNCR: Try Four-Season Climate Control…or Cadillac Comfort Control. Enjoy wonderful weather wherever you drive…the ideal temperature inside your car every day of the year. GM Harrison Four-Season Climate Control is available on Chevrolets, Pontiacs, Oldsmobiles and Buicks—most of the smaller-size models, too. Ask for a demonstration at your General Motors Dealers.

PREAM COMMERCIALS

60-second radio spot for Pream, approved by the ad agency, 9-6-66.

(SNORING SOUNDS. BIRDS CHIRPING IN BKGD.)

BLANCHE: John Bickerson! Will you put that fishing pole down long enough to taste this coffee I made for you?

JOHN: Uh. Uh. Where izze? Whereizze?

BLANCHE: Where's *who*?

JOHN: Big Sam. I've been tryin' to hook that fish for eight years and this year I'm gonna do it.

BLANCHE: In your *sleep*?

JOHN: I wasn't asleep, Blanche. Don't ya recognize a *fish call* when you hear one? I was *luring* Big Sam.

BLANCHE: Well, forget about that fish for a minute and taste this coffee. It's got a surprise in it.

JOHN: *Bour*bon?

BLANCHE: No, *Pream*. I packed it for the trip. And wait'll you taste it. New Pream tastes even better than cream.

JOHN: Okay, Blanche. Hand me the coffee and I'll—

(SUDDEN WHIRRING OF REEL, WATER SPLASHING.)

Blanche! It's Big Sam! I've hooked Big Sam! (MORE SPLASHING, WHIRRING) Watch out! Hang on, Big Sam! Oh, no! He got away—I've *lost him*!

BLANCHE: Oh, darn! You spilled the coffee, John. Now you won't get to taste New Pream.

JOHN: Pream! *Pream*! (SOBBING) *What about Big Sam*!!!

BLANCHE: Well, he can't go far, John. After all, he *is* in the lake. All you have to do is *catch* him.

JOHN: (PITIFUL GROAN)

ANNCR: Try New Pream. It really does taste better than cream.

"RED CABBAGE" (60 SECONDS)

SOUND:	(CLATTER OF DISHES)
JOHN:	(SNORES LIGHTLY)
BLANCHE:	John Bickerson, wake up!
JOHN:	Uhuh… uhuh.. Whatsamatter, Blanche?
BLANCHE:	How can you sleep at the breakfast table?
JOHN:	It's my only defense against your cooking.
BLANCHE:	What's wrong with my cooking?
JOHN:	Look at these! Whoever heard of purple pancakes!
BLANCHE:	Those aren't pancakes, John. That's a *red cabbage omelet*.
JOHN:	For breakfast?
BLANCHE:	Well, you don't like the *normal* things people eat for breakfast…
JOHN:	I like normal breakfasts, Blanche. You just don't know how to make 'em that way!
BLANCHE:	Oh John, I try so hard to make everything nice. I even fixed your coffee a different way this morning.
JOHN:	Didn't burn it, huh?
BLANCHE:	I put Pream in it, John. Pream tastes better than cream in your coffee.
JOHN:	Maybe it'll drown out the taste altogether.
BLANCHE:	You never appreciate anything I do! I used New Pream especially for you. Now you better taste it, John Bickerson! Go ahead. *Taste* it!
JOHN:	Alright, Blanche. (PAUSE. RATTLE OF SPOON AGAINST GLASS) E-yech! Kinda dry, isn't it?
BLANCHE:	Not from the jar, stupid. In the coffee!
ANNCR:	Try New Pream. It really does taste better than cream.

"BREAKFAST TABLE" (60 SECONDS)

SOUND:	(TINKLE OF CUP & SAUCER, RATTLE OF NEWSPAPER)
BLANCHE:	Jo-ohn…?

JOHN:	Umph.
BLANCHE.	John?
JOHN:	Umph.
BLANCHE:	John Bickerson, will you get your head out of that newspaper! Every morning it's the same! You never pay any attention to me!
JOHN:	Mph.
BLANCHE:	(SWEETLY) John, guess what I put in your coffee this morning?
JOHN:	Mph.
BLANCHE:	Catsup!
JOHN:	Mph. (PAUSE) What did you say, Blanche?
BLANCHE:	I said I put catsup in your coffee.
JOHN:	Blanche, you know I like my coffee black.
BLANCHE:	Actually, I put some Pream in your coffee. And it's delicious. It actually improves the taste.
JOHN:	Blanche, nothing can improve the taste of your coffee.
BLANCHE:	Well, this does. New Pream tastes even better than cream.
JOHN:	Okay, okay—I'll try it, just for you.
	(PAUSE. SLURPING SOUNDS)
BLANCHE:	Well?
JOHN:	(SLURP) Tastes just like always. Sweet and sticky.
BLANCHE:	That's not the coffee! That's the pancake syrup!
JOHN:	Well, can I help it if you—
BLANCHE:	You never appreciate me! You never pay any—
JOHN:	(FADING OUT) Blanche, I don't even like breakfast—
ANNCR:	Try New Pream. It really does taste better than cream.

"FIVE O'CLOCK" (60 SECONDS)

SOUND:	(SNORING SOUNDS. MORE SNORING SOUNDS)
BLANCHE:	John…Wake up, John.
JOHN:	Uh! Uh-uh! Whatsamatter! Whatsamatter!

BLANCHE: I want you to taste this coffee, John.

JOHN: Coffee? Coffee! Blanche, it's five o'clock in the morning! I don't need coffee! I need sleep!

BLANCHE: I couldn't help it, John. I've made a discovery and I'm so excited about it, I couldn't wait. I had to share it with you.

JOHN: Blanche—I share your bed. I share your cooking. I even share your mother! Do I haveta share your discoveries, too? (RESIGNED) Okay, what is it?

BLANCHE: It's New Pream, John. I ran out of cream so I used this Pream in the coffee instead. And it's delicious. Here, taste it.

JOHN: Pream, cream, schmeem. It's five o'clock in the morning, Blanche!

BLANCHE: *Taste* it, John. New Pream tastes even better than cream!

JOHN: Okay, gimme the coffee.

(PAUSE. SLURPING SOUNDS)

BLANCHE: Well?

JOHN: I can't taste a thing. The coffee's cold.

BLANCHE: *Cold?* Well if you wouldn't take so long—

JOHN: Blanche, all I said was—

BLANCHE: You never appreciate me! You never—

JOHN: Blanche, it's five o'clock in the morning—(FADE UNDER ANNCR)

ANNCR: Try New Pream in your coffee. It really does taste better than cream.

"SPOON" (60 SECONDS)

BLANCHE: (SOFTLY) John, oh John, I have something for you.

JOHN: I'll bet!

BLANCHE: Something new to drink.

JOHN: I could use a drink.

BLANCHE: It's coffee with New Pream in it. It tastes better than cream.

JOHN: Well, your coffee could use some help.

BLANCHE: What did you say, John?

JOHN:	Nothing, Blanche.
BLANCHE:	Come on. Say it. You hate my cooking, don't you?
JOHN:	I don't hate it, Blanche, I just don't understand it.
BLANCHE:	Here I spend the best years of my life trying to please you. Buy you Pream. Pream because it tastes better than cream in your coffee. Even saves you money. Mother was right.
JOHN:	All right, Blanche, I'll try your Pream.
BLANCHE:	You say it but you won't do it. Do it now, John.
JOHN:	Agh…
BLANCHE:	You've got to take the spoon out of the cup first, stupid.
ANNCR:	Try New Pream. It really does taste better than cream.

"CHECKBOOK" (60 SECONDS)

SOUND:	(SOUND OF DOOR SLAMMING)
BLANCHE:	John-n-n, I'm home! Look John, I bought a new hat and…
JOHN:	Wait a minute, Blanche. Can't you see I'm busy? (HE MUMBLES) 45 minus 56 minus…
BLANCHE:	And gloves and shoes…
JOHN:	Holy Moses!
BLANCHE:	—and a purse and…
JOHN:	Blanche! You've done it again! Our checkbook is shot full of holes! Money gone with the wind!
BLANCHE:	That's just what happened.
JOHN:	Oh no! The poorhouse!
BLANCHE:	But I needed new accessories.
JOHN:	Yeah, and I'll be accessory to a crime, when the bank gets that check!
BLANCHE:	John! I'm threadbare! I always look as poor as a churchmouse.
JOHN:	Here. Have some Swiss cheese.
BLANCHE:	Well, cheer up, John. How about some coffee and New Pream.
JOHN:	How about saving some money for a change?

BLANCHE: Pream not only tastes better than cream, it's lots cheaper than cream.

JOHN: It'll take five years of using Pream to pay for everything you bought.

BLANCHE: I know. That's why I bought a five-year supply.

ANNCR: Try New Pream. It really does taste better than cream.

RTA COMMERCIAL

ANNCR: R.T.A. presents Don Ameche and Frances Langford as THE BICKERSONS!

DON: (SNORES LUSTILY...SNORES AND WHINES)

FRAN: That's enough, John! Up, up, up!

DON: What's up, Blanche?

FRAN: You are! Time to come alive and get to work.

DON: Don't have to be at the cemetery till nine—thirty-minute drive.

FRAN: No more driving, John—from now on you take the train. Haven't you heard about the energy crisis?

DON: (STILL HALF ASLEEP) Mmm.

FRAN: Didn't you know there's a terrific lack of energy?

DON: No.

FRAN: You should—you're the Midwest distributor of it!

DON: Very funny.

FRAN: What time did you get home last night?

DON: Late.

FRAN: You didn't pass a cocktail bar on the way, did you?

DON: (FULLY AWAKE) I NEVER pass a cocktail bar!

FRAN: How well I know it! How many drinks did you have?

DON: I didn't have any!

FRAN: Then why are you trying to put your pants on over your head?

DON: What pants? This is the sweater you made for me out of your old slacks. I'm the only man alive with a V-neck seat!

FRAN: Well, stop throwing your things around for me to pick up. You think I'm a vacuum cleaner?

DON: No, Blanche—a vacuum cleaner can be shut off! Get my lunch!

FRAN: Here—take this limburger sandwich.

DON: Okay. Bye.

FRAN: Hold it—how about a kiss?

DON: (KISSES LIKE MAD)

FRAN: ME—not the sandwich. Oh—goodbye!

ANNCR: No need to spend your life fighting traffic or bad weather on the highways to get to work. Take the RTA—twice a day. In a year you could save up to $2,000—and maybe an ulcer.

XMAS SHOW
REVISED
JULY 14, 1970

THE BICKERSONS

Created and Written
by
PHILIP RAPP

FADE IN:

FULL SHOT – BUSY STREET – DAY

It is winter. Assorted characters are moving purposefully in both directions, some carrying packages, some lugging Christmas trees, some entering and exiting a large store with a window full of toys and gifts. The lettering above the window proclaims the store to be TINKER'S TOY EMPORIUM. Directly in front of the store stands a SALVATION ARMY SANTA CLAUS ringing his bell beside the traditional pot. By this time the viewer should get the general idea. Christmas is upon us.

                                      DISSOLVE:

FULL SHOT – RESIDENTIAL STREET

The CAMERA PANS ALONG a row of nondescript houses, some bedecked with holly wreaths and other seasonal ornaments, and comes to rest on the two-story frame house occupied by JOHN and BLANCHE BICKERSON and Blanche's sister CLARA, her husband HARVEY and their girl child, LITTLE DARLING. This family, THE DOLLOPS, occupies the upper portion of the house. (I must assume that the TITLES will be supered over the foregoing.)

                                      DISSOLVE:

INT. BICKERSON APARTMENT – BEDROOM

JOHN is asleep, SNORING HUGELY. BLANCHE enters, listens for a beat or two to the snoring and whining and giggling, then shakes her head.

                       BLANCHE
          It's like living with a one-man band!

She moves over to the bed and leans over John.

> BLANCHE (cont'd)
> John! John Bickerson! Wake up!

> JOHN
> Huh? Wassamatter, Blanche?

> BLANCHE
> You'll be late for work.

> JOHN (mumbling)
> Not going to work…

> BLANCHE
> Of course you are! Your boss will be furious if you don't show up.

> JOHN
> Tell him I'm sick…
> (groans)
> Ohhhh, Blanche, go look at my birth certificate and see if it expired…

He gets up slowly, moaning softly and holding his head. Blanche looks at him with no sympathy.

> BLANCHE
> Serves you right if you don't feel well. Who told you to drink all that bourbon at the office party last night?

> JOHN
> Nobody told me and I didn't drink all that bourbon.

> BLANCHE
> I married a great big corkscrew!

> JOHN
> You cut that out! You know as well as I do that drinking is not one of my failures.

> BLANCHE
> No—it's one of your few successes!

> JOHN
> The only reason I use a little bourbon is because Dr. Hersey

prescribed it. He said it would help me sleep if I took a jigger of bourbon and two aspirins every night.

                BLANCHE
That's not what you do though.

                JOHN
Yes, it is.

                BLANCHE
It is not! You're six months behind on the aspirin and two years ahead on the bourbon.

                JOHN
Well, aspirin gives me a headache.

                BLANCHE
Oh, go take a shower and pull yourself together. Go on.

He staggers into the connecting bathroom as Blanche does a quick job of making the bed then starts out of the bedroom. From o.s. there is the SOUND of RUNNING WATER, then, suddenly, a fiendish yell.

                JOHN'S VOICE
Yeowwwwwwww!

INT. BATHROOM

John dashes out of the shower, still wearing his pyjamas! He's soaked to the skin, and he's standing there shivering and shaking and *literally turning blue* as Blanche rushes in.

                WIPE:

                BLANCHE
Harvey's entitled to all the hot water he wants! He and Clara are tenants in this house!

                JOHN
Yeah? It's been six months since that mooch paid me any rent!

                BLANCHE
Don't worry. Harvey's good for it.
  (starts out)
Now try the shower again, John. I'm going to fix you some breakfast.

INT. DOLLOP'S APARTMENT

HARVEY is seated at a dining table polishing off a huge platter of food. LITTLE DARLING is staring at him, fascinated. He stops eating.

> HARVEY (mouth full)
> Stop staring at me like that.

> L. D.
> Why?

> HARVEY
> Never mind why. Go play with your friends, Little Darling.

> LITTLE DARLING
> I only got one friend—and I hate her.

> HARVEY
> Well, go play on the freeway.

> L. D.
> I don't wanna.

CLARA enters.

> CLARA
> Harvey, I'm worried. John's dunning us for the rent.

> HARVEY
> John?

> CLARA
> John Bickerson—your brother-in-law.

> HARVEY
> You mean *your* brother-in-law. I wouldn't have him for a second cousin!

> CLARA
> That's beside the point. He owns this house and he wants his rent.

> HARVEY
> Tell him I can't pay it this month.

CLARA
That's what you told him last month.

HARVEY
Well, I kept my word, didn't I?

CLARA
You can't keep sneaking past him every morning—

HARVEY
Quit bugging me, Clara! When I've got the money I'll pay him—and besides what's he need it for anyway?

CLARA
He wants to buy Blanche a Christmas present and he needs some extra money.

HARVEY
He needs extra money, let him get an extra job.

CLARA
What kind of job?

HARVEY
Don't ask me. I don't know anything about working. I'm an executive!
(hands her empty plate)
More pastrami and corned-beef sandwiches, Clara. And this time go heavy on the mayonnaise.

WIPE TO:

INT. KITCHEN

John, now dressed in overalls, comes to the table, looks at the food, pushes the plate away.

BLANCHE
Why don't you eat your breakfast?

JOHN
Take it away.

BLANCHE
Go ahead, pick on my cooking. You won't eat this, you won't eat that—

JOHN
Well, I won't eat *that*! I'm going out and work on the car.

BLANCHE
What for?

JOHN
I'm gonna try and sell it—I need some extra money for a special reason.

BLANCHE
Sure. Probably to squander it on more bour—

JOHN
Now don't start that again!

BLANCHE
You sit down and eat first. There's nothing wrong with that broccoli rice pudding.

JOHN
I've told you a million times, Blanche—I can't stand the sight of rice!

BLANCHE
Why not?

JOHN
Because it's connected with one of the saddest mistakes of my life!

BLANCHE
Too bad about you, John Bickerson. I didn't get such a bargain, either. There are better fish in the ocean than the one I caught!

JOHN
There's better bait, too!

BLANCHE
I'd love to hear you talk like that to Gloria Gooseby!

JOHN
Now don't start with Gloria Gooseby.

BLANCHE
Believe me, if you were married to her she wouldn't let you get away with anything.

JOHN
I'm not married to her and she lets me get away with everything!

BLANCHE
What!

JOHN
I mean, I hate the sight of Gloria Gooseby and I never want you to mention her name again—you hear me!

BLANCHE
Stop yelling. Harvey just finished breakfast upstairs, and he's taking a nap.

JOHN
Yeah, he must really be exhausted—eating and breathing all the time…

BLANCHE
Why do you dislike Harvey so, John?

JOHN
Dislike? I don't dislike him, Blanche.
(viciously)
I hate him—I loathe him—and unless I see that rent money today, I'm evicting all of them!

BLANCHE
How can you talk like that? In other words, you'd throw my sister and their beautiful child out on the street?

JOHN
No, those are the exact words!

He reaches for a bowl of food.

BLANCHE
You're worse than Scrooge. Here it is three days before Christmas and you want to dispossess my relatives.

JOHN (eating)
If that crook doesn't pay me I can't pay the mortgage. I've got a ninety dollar equity in this house and I don't want them to foreclose.

> BLANCHE
> Did you ever hear of the milk of human kindness?

> JOHN
> Pass the milk.

> BLANCHE
> Very funny. Well, for your information, Harvey's going to be a very rich man. He's got a big deal cooking.

John feels something at his leg, looks down and sees the cat pulling at his pants.

> JOHN
> Get out of here! What does that cat want from me, Blanche?

> BLANCHE
> Nothing. It's just that you're eating out of his bowl.

> WIPE

INT. TINKER'S TOY EMPORIUM

It's every child's dream of a toy store—and, since it's nearly Christmas, it's loaded with customers. The MANAGER is walking toward the entrance with the store SANTA CLAUS, who is taking off his beard and shirt and pillow and pants, etc., as he goes. In the b.g. we can SEE a SLED and EIGHT PLASTIC REINDEERS set up with a sign overhead, SANTA'S SLED, and in a line of kids standing watching the Santa go.

> MANAGER
> But you can't quit now! Those children need a Santa Claus!

EXT. TINKER'S TOY EMPORIUM

As the Santa and Manager come out, Harvey is passing by. He stops and watches the scene with interest.

> SANTA
> They don't need a Santa Claus, they need a punching bag!!
> And I can't drive that crazy sled either!

He marches off. Harvey approaches the Manager.

> HARVEY
> Excuse me—are you in the market for a real good Santa Claus?

MANAGER
You're too skinny.

HARVEY
Not me—a friend of mine. Very experienced man. Sweet, gentle, jovial—and kids just love him. And I'm sure he can handle that sled. Used to be a jet pilot.

MANAGER
Okay—send him over. What's his name?

HARVEY
John Bickerson.

DISSOLVE:

INT. GARAGE

John is working underneath the Bickerson car—a very old model. Just his feet can be seen. Blanche enters the garage.

BLANCHE
John.

JOHN'S VOICE (over hammering)
Wait a minute, Blanche.

BLANCHE
Come out from under there. I've got to talk to you.

He crawls out from under the car pretty smeared up. He remains on his back.

JOHN
What do you want?

BLANCHE
Where's Nature Boy?

JOHN
Who's Nature Boy?

BLANCHE
The cat. I haven't seen him since you upset him when you ate out of his bowl. I think he ran off.

JOHN
He didn't run off—he's under the car with me.

He points under the car. Blanche bends down to look.

P.O.V. – CAT UNDER CAR

He is a sorry mess. Not the golden-coated cat we saw before, but a black, bedraggled tom.

> BLANCHE
> That black alley cat isn't ours! Nature Boy has a golden coat.

> JOHN
> That's him. I've been petting him.

> BLANCHE
> You mean you've been wiping your hands on him!

> JOHN
> Okay—so I've been wiping my hands on him. I couldn't find a rag.

> BLANCHE
> You ought to be ashamed of yourself. Look at the poor thing—he looks like he fell in a tar pit.

> JOHN
> Well, he had no right to come sniffing around while I was draining the oil. Put him in the washing machine.

> BLANCHE
> I will not! And you stop using Nature Boy for a grease rag. How long are you going to be working on that pile of junk?

> JOHN
> Till I get it fixed.

> BLANCHE
> You finally steal some time off from work and how do you spend it? Under a car.

> JOHN (gets up, oil can in hand)
> I'm happy here. Before you came out it was nice and quiet.

> BLANCHE
> Stop waving that oil can around—it's pouring all over the car. Wipe it up, John.

JOHN
Okay—hand me the cat.

BLANCHE
You leave him alone! How much longer are you going to be?

JOHN
I'm almost through. Grab hold of that wire, will you, Blanche.

BLANCHE (grasping wire under hood)
This one?

JOHN
Yeah—feel anything?

BLANCHE
No—why?

JOHN
Nothing. I just wanted to see if it was connected to the battery.

BLANCHE
John Bickerson!

JOHN
Oh, take it easy—the battery's dead, anyway. I gotta have it recharged.

Harvey enters the scene.

HARVEY
Oh, there you are, John! I've been looking all over for you.

BLANCHE
Hi, Harvey.

JOHN (holding out his hand)
The rent, please.

HARVEY
Yes. Well, I—

JOHN
The rent, Harvey!

> HARVEY (feeling in his pockets)
> Darn it! I must have left my wallet upstairs.

> JOHN
> Blanche, go upstairs and ask your sister if Harvey's wallet is there. And don't you move, Harvey.

Blanche leaves.

> HARVEY
> I can't understand why you're so suspicious, John. As a matter of fact, I came to offer you something much more valuable than the rent.

> JOHN
> Uh-huh.

> HARVEY
> You see, I've just opened an employment agency and—

> JOHN
> I've got a job.

> HARVEY
> A bowling ball salesman? Is that what you want to be all your life?

> JOHN
> It pays the rent—which is more than you do.

> HARVEY
> If you keep harping on that I may consider moving.

> JOHN
> You may—?

> HARVEY
> Now, listen to me, John. For a small fee I can secure a position for you—

> JOHN
> I told you I've got a job!

> HARVEY
> You want some extra money to buy Blanche a Christmas present, don't you?

JOHN (taking the bait)
What's this job? Where is it?

HARVEY
Ever hear of Tinker's Toy Emporium? Well, I just had a talk with the owner and they need a man to take charge.

JOHN
Take charge?

HARVEY (hands him a card)
Get dressed and go see Mr. Tucker right away. Tell him your name and tell him I sent you.

JOHN
Harvey, if there's something fishy—

HARVEY
If there is, I'll give you your hundred dollars back.

JOHN
What hundred dollars?

HARVEY
My fee. I'm only charging you half because you're my brother-in-law—but you can make it up by calling off the rent. Sign here.

Hands him a form.

JOHN
Hey, wait a minute—

Blanche enters.

BLANCHE
Clara says she can't find your wallet, Harvey.

HARVEY
No? Well, go help John look for his. We just made a deal and he owes me some money.

On John's bewildered reaction

DISSOLVE:

INT. BICKERSON APARTMENT - BEDROOM

John is changing his clothes as Blanche bustles about, helping.

> JOHN
> I tell you, Blanche—this whole thing is a big con. Why did you give Harvey the money?

> BLANCHE
> You'll get it back a hundred times over. You listen to Harvey—I've got confidence in that man.

> JOHN
> Confidence man is right.

> BLANCHE
> He's a genius. You know as well as I do that when he lived in Canada he was knighted for his operations in the stock market.

> JOHN
> It was the black market—and he wasn't knighted—he was indicted! Knighted!

> BLANCHE
> What's the difference—he found you a wonderful job and I think you should call up your old boss—that Mr. Cleaver—

> JOHN
> Carver!

> BLANCHE
> Carver—whatever—and tell him what he can do with his filthy old job.

> JOHN
> Now, wait a minute—

> BLANCHE
> Take off that tie—it doesn't go with that green suit. I'll go get another one.

She exits. John takes off his tie, and quite mechanically, due to years of exhaustion, takes off his coat, shirt, pants, shoes, etc.—and remains standing in his underwear, eyes closing. He falls into bed and starts to snore as Blanche enters with a tie and reacts violently.

FADE OUT

FADE IN:

INT. BICKERSON APARTMENT

Clara and L. D. are with Blanche in the kitchen. Harvey is at the ice-box rummaging for food.

> CLARA
> Leave that stuff alone, Harvey—it's for the celebration tonight.

> HARVEY
> What celebration?

> L. D.
> What celebration?

> JOHN
> The big job you got for John. At Tinker's Toy Emporium.

> L. D.
> I wanna go there. Take me to Stinker's Toy Emporium, Daddy.

> CLARA
> Yes, why don't you take her, Harvey? She can see Santa Claus there.

> HARVEY (a jolt)
> Santa Claus—no. No, I can't take her—I got an important appointment.

> L. D.
> I wanna go to Stinker's and see Santa Claus!

> BLANCHE
> Why don't you take her, Clara? Just ask for John and she might not even have to stand in line like the other kids.

Harvey grabs a chicken leg and runs out.

> CLARA (looking after him)
> Now what do you suppose got into him?

DISSOLVE:

EXT. TINKER'S TOY EMPORIUM

As John pulls himself together, assumes an air of dignity and strides in.

DISSOLVE:

INT. OFFICE

John sits opposite Mr. Tinker, the owner. He is the man we saw firing Santa Claus.

          TINKER
This job requires great patience and diplomacy. Children can be very demanding.

          JOHN
Children?

          TINKER
After all—we're a toy store. Don't you like children?

          JOHN
Oh, sure. I love 'em. I've got a niece who lives in the same house with us. Pretty repulsive kid. I mean impulsive.

          TINKER
Yes. I hope your habits are regular. Do you drink anything?

          JOHN
Anything.

          TINKER
What's that?

          JOHN
Anything you say I'm willing to do, Mr. Tinker. When do I start?

          TINKER
Right now. You might find the hours rather long—but you'll be sitting down all the time.

          JOHN
Fine, fine.

          TINKER
Just be careful when you hold the girls on your lap.

JOHN
Girls on my lap? You mean I have more than one secretary?

TINKER (laughs)
I'm going to be pleased with you, Bickerson—you have a fine sense of humor. Well, you'd better run along to the locker room and take off those clothes.

JOHN (startled)
What?

TINKER (handing him Santa Claus suit and beard)
Here—put these on and stuff a pillow under the coat.

JOHN (in dismay)
You mean—you mean—

TINKER (smiling)
Exactly. Merry Christmas, Santa.

John almost passes out.

DISSOLVE:

INT. TINKER'S

John Bickerson, a very unhappy Santa Claus, sits on the seat of the sleigh, a little BOY on his lap. Lined up waiting for a chance to talk to him is a FLOCK OF KIDS.

JOHN (a disgusted look on his face)
Is that all?

BOY
No. And I want a motorcycle and a guitar and some love beads and and Indian headband and some sandals.

JOHN
No pot?

BOY
Huh?

JOHN
Okay, scram! (pushes him off lap)
A six-year-old hippie! Next!

Clara enters with L. D. and they survey the long line.

> CLARA
> You get on line, Little Darling, and I'll go look for Uncle John.

She exits. Little Darling looks at the size of the line, then notes that the current lap-sitter is crying piteously.

> CRYING KID
> Take me home, Mommy—I don't like that ugly man—he scares me!

L.D. has now worked her way up to the front of the line.

> L. D. (jumping on John's lap)
> He don't scare me, little boy. It's not a real Santa Claus—there ain't no Santa Claus!

> CRYING KID
> There is, too!

> L. D.
> Oh, no, there ain't! It's like the devil—it's your father! Look, I'll show you he ain't real!

She reaches up to pull off his beard, and John grapples with her. As they fight and grapple, John AD-LIBBING "Cut it out," etc., we

CUT TO:

INSERT SHOT – ROCKET ACTIVATOR BUTTON INSIDE SLEIGH

Little Darling accidentally hits the button.

BACK TO SCENE

As the rockets which propel the sleigh suddenly fire into life and the sleigh starts forward.

> JOHN
> Hey! Wait! How do you stop this thing??

L. D. looks around, then smiles.

> L. D. (happy)
> I wanna drive! I wanna drive!

By this time the sleigh has picked up speed and is careening through the store, knocking over expensive toy displays, felling customers, etc.

TWO SHOT – CLARA AND TINKER.

> TINKER
> Of course I can show you to Mr. Bickerson, Mrs. Dollop. If you'll just come this way I'll—

He's cut off by the riotous commotion and then reacts, horrified.

NEW ANGLE

As the sleigh bearing John and Little Darling roars toward them.

> TINKER
> Oh, no…

The sleigh zooms over Clara and Tinker, causing them to drop to the ground, and heads right toward the front door of the emporium. The sleigh zooms out the door, heading up.

> CLARA
> My baby! He just flew off with my little girl!

> TINKER
> Little girls can be replaced! That sleigh cost three hundred dollars!

EXT. SKY – DAY

The sleigh is flying along high over the city. John is hanging on for dear life, while Little Darling manipulates the controls, loving every minute of it.

P.O.V. SHOT – THE CITY

From above.

BACK TO SCENE

The reindeer and sleigh perform some incredible maneuvers.

> L. D.
> Wheeeee!
> (to John who is turning green)
> Which way to the North Pole, Santa?

MED. SHOT – HELICOPTER

A traffic-monitor helicopter.

INT. HELICOPTER

The PILOT is looking down, talking into a microphone.

> PILOT
> And so, folks, this is your WXKR traffic-copter turning you back to Top-Forty Ferdie and wishing you Christmas Cheer!!

He clicks off his mike as ROCK MUSIC now fills the copter. Suddenly, the pilot looks o.s.

HIS P.O.V. – THE SLEIGH

flying past him.

BACK TO SCENE

As he stares, then picks up the mike, speaks low.

> PILOT
> Ferdie…it's me…You're not gonna believe this, but I just saw Santa Claus and his reindeer fly by me in a sleigh…
>
> FERDIE'S VOICE (over radio)
> Yeah? Better go easy on that Christmas cheer, Lucky…

WIPE TO:

INT. MR. CARVER'S OFFICE - ACME BOWLING BALL COMPANY

MR. CARVER (John's boss) is in his office at the Acme Bowling Ball Company talking to his grandson, EUSTACE.

> EUSTACE
> But, Grandpa, you promised you'd take me to see Santa Claus…
>
> MR. CARVER
> I know I did, my dear. But Christmas is our biggest bowling ball season, and one of my salesmen, John Bickerson, is home ill, so I just can't get away.

> EUSTACE (starts to cry)
> But, Grandpa, you promised…

CUT TO:

EXT. SKY

The sleigh takes a sharp nose-dive and starts plunging downward. John covers his eyes, but L. D. is really digging it.

> L. D.
> Wheeeeee! I guess we're going to the *South* Pole, huh, Santa?

CUT TO:

INT. CARVER'S OFFICE

Eustace is crying.

> CARVER
> Eustace, dear, please try to understand that I can't take you to see Santa Claus because—

He's cut off by a HUGE CRASH from o.s. Carver rushes out, way ahead of the sobbing Eustace.

CUT TO:

INT. MAIN BOWLING PIN STOCKROOM

The sleigh has crashed through the roof, and there, amidst a ton of bowling pins, sits John, beard askew, and L. D., grinning widely.

> CARVER (entering)
> What in—(sees John)
> Bickerson! I thought you were sick!

> JOHN (woefully)
> I am now. And I wish I were dead!

> CARVER (furious)
> You faker! Calling up and saying you were sick—
> taking another job—destroying my plant—
> (moves to John menacingly)
> When I get through with you—

Eustace, still sobbing, has entered, and when he sees "Santa" he suddenly lights up.

> EUSTACE
> Oh, Grandpa, you did it! You got me to see Santa Claus after all!

> CARVER
> What? Well, errr, I—that is—

> JOHN (grabbing the straw)
> Ho-ho-ho! Your grandfather certainly is a wonderful man, isn't he, little boy? Ho-ho-ho! Take him out and play house with him, Little Darling.

L. D. grabs Eustace and they exit.

> CARVER
> That was quick thinking, Bickerson. Sorry I hollered. Matter of fact, I think you deserve a reward.

> JOHN
> A reward?

> CARVER
> Seeing as how you bailed me out with my grandson, I'm not going to make you pay for the damage you've done.

> JOHN
> You're not??

> CARVER
> No. I'm just going to cut your salary in half, for a year. Merry Christmas, Bickerson.

John slumps down, dejected, as a final bowling pin falls from a shelf onto his head.

DISSOLVE TO:

INT. BICKERSON BEDROOM - NIGHT

Blanche is in her nightgown sitting on the bed, just hanging up the phone. The door opens and a dishevelled Santa Claus, minus beard, enters.

> BLANCHE
> John! It's past midnight. Where have you been—and why are you wearing that outfit?

JOHN (burning)
Where's that Harvey? I'll kill him. Where is he?

BLANCHE
He took Clara and Little Darling and they went for a holiday.

JOHN
With my money! That thief! I told you he was a phoney! This is the job he got me!

He tears off his clothes and is revealed undressed in pyjamas. He goes straight to his bed. The cat is under the covers. He throws him out.

JOHN (cont'd)
Put out the light.

BLANCHE
Where have you been so long?

JOHN
If you must know, I was down at night court.

BLANCHE
Night court!

JOHN
Yes. I got picked up for parking in a loading zone.

BLANCHE
What were you doing in a loading zone?

JOHN
I was loading! Satisfied? Is that what you wanted to hear?

BLANCHE
No. You might have called me. I left some dinner for you in the kitchen.

JOHN
Good. Put out the lights. I'm dead tired.

BLANCHE
That's because you don't eat enough. You lie there—I'll bring in the stuff I made for you.

She exits to kitchen. Nature Boy comes back to bed and tries the snuggle in with John. He throws the cat out again. Blanche returns with a plate of food, offers it to John. He stares at it.

> JOHN
> Blanche, would you mind telling me what's on this plate?
>
> BLANCHE
> Are you trying to be funny, John?
>
> JOHN
> I'm not trying to be funny, Blanche. What is it?
>
> BLANCHE
> You know very well I can only cook two things—liver and rice pudding.
>
> JOHN
> Well, which one is this?
>
> BLANCHE
> How can you be so nasty when it's so close to Christmas, John?
>
> JOHN
> I just asked you a civil question, that's all. I didn't think it was liver because your liver always looks like rubber heels—but this stuff looks more like wallpaper paste so I thought it might be rice pudding.
>
> BLANCHE
> Why don't you taste it and find out?
>
> JOHN
> I don't want it.

He puts the plate on the dresser and gets in bed.

> BLANCHE
> Nothing I do for you is any good. I spent three hours in the kitchen preparing that mess and you complain about it.
>
> JOHN
> I'm not complaining. I'm just not hungry!
>
> BLANCHE
> You always pick at your food and you never say you like it.

JOHN
I always say I like it. You're a wonderful cook!

BLANCHE
Then why do you keep getting ptomaine poisoning?

JOHN
Go figure that one out. Go to sleep, Blanche.

BLANCHE
I'm not going to sleep until you say something nice to me.

JOHN
Oh dear.

BLANCHE
This is the Christmas season and it's almost heathen the way we carry on. You can be sweet if you want.

JOHN
Mmm.

BLANCHE
Go on, John—say something soft and sweet.

JOHN
Banana pudding.

BLANCHE
That isn't a bit funny! It won't kill you to pay me a tiny compliment.

JOHN
What do you want me to say, Blanche?

BLANCHE
Say I look beautiful.

JOHN
I look beautiful—goodnight.

BLANCHE
Isn't it strange how unromantic a man can be after eight years of marriage.

JOHN
Nothing strange about it.

BLANCHE
Before we were married you used to say such beautiful poetic things. You don't anymore.

JOHN
Blanche, how do you expect me to feel poetic at two o'clock in the morning?

BLANCHE
You used to feel that way at five o'clock! Say something poetic.

JOHN
Humpty-dumpty sat on a wall—
Humpty-dumpty had a great—

BLANCHE
Oh, stop it! You're just trying to irritate me now!

JOHN
Well, I don't know what you want.

BLANCHE
Just tell me you love me and you'll never stop loving me.

JOHN
I love you. I'll love you as long as the moon is glowing—as long as the stars are twinkling—I'll love you as long as the sun is shining. Satisfied?

BLANCHE
No.

JOHN
Why not?

BLANCHE
You'll only love me as long as the weather is nice.

JOHN
Oh, this is awful. I'm dying for a few minutes sleep and you're running me ragged!

BLANCHE
Well, why didn't you come home earlier and trim the Christmas tree?

JOHN
Plenty of time for that.

BLANCHE
No, there isn't. I expect a lot of people to drop in tomorrow. The milkman is coming, the grocer is coming, the butcher is coming—

JOHN
Listen, Blanche, I can't afford to give those chisellers any presents! Why did you invite them?

BLANCHE
I didn't invite them. They're coming to collect their bills.

JOHN
Bills! Bills! I don't know how I'm gonna live through this Christmas.

BLANCHE
Listen to me, John. You get up and trim the tree right now and see if it doesn't make you feel better.

He struggles out of bed, goes to the closet and brings out a scrawny, two-foot tree. He sets it down. Then he gets some decorations from the dresser. He hangs one glass ball on, showers a box of snow over it and stares at it.

JOHN
It's kinda small—but I didn't have anymore money to spare, Blanche.

BLANCHE
Don't you worry, darling—it looks fine. I hope the cat doesn't drag it under the sink like he did last year.

JOHN
I hope not.

BLANCHE
Now don't go back to bed—I have a surprise for you. Just close your eyes.

She gets up and goes to the kitchen and comes out wheeling a brand new, small portable bar.

> BLANCHE (cont'd)
> Open your eyes, John.

John opens his eyes and is stunned.

> JOHN
> Blanche! Oh, Blanche! It's beautiful! It's a dream. A portable bar—with a brass rail!

> BLANCHE
> That's my present to you.

> JOHN
> Oh, Blanche darling, it's wonderful.

> BLANCHE
> Don't you think a kiss is in order, John?

> JOHN
> A million kisses!

He kisses the bar fervently.

> BLANCHE
> I mean a kiss for me.

> JOHN
> I'm sorry, dearest—it's too good to be true.
> (kisses her cheek)
> You're wonderful, Blanche, it must have cost a fortune.

> BLANCHE
> John, don't get angry—but I sold my fur coat.

> JOHN
> You sold your fur coat?

> BLANCHE
> I wanted you to have the bar—and I didn't have the money.

> JOHN
> You sold your coat? That beautiful fur coat that you bought yourself for my birthday? That gorgeous bald mink?

BLANCHE
I got seventy dollars for it. The bar cost eighty-five.

JOHN
Oh, Blanche—you never should have sold that bald mink.

BLANCHE
It doesn't matter. I have a cloth coat—and I never get cold.

JOHN
But you don't understand—

He goes to the closet and brings out a box.

JOHN (cont'd)
Open it.

She opens the box and takes out a fur muff.

BLANCHE
Ohhhh! A muff. A beautiful fur muff.

JOHN
Genuine plucked skunk. I had it made especially to match that coat of yours. It can hold two full quarts and you sold the coat.

BLANCHE
What's the difference, darling? Someday you'll make a lot of money and then you can buy me a coat to match the muff. I'm very happy, John.

JOHN
I know, but—but—

BLANCHE
And you still have this lovely bar.

JOHN
That's just it.

BLANCHE
What's the matter?

JOHN
I sold all my bourbon to pay for the muff. That's great, isn't it? What a break for both of us.

BLANCHE
I think it's wonderful, John.

JOHN
Wonderful.

BLANCHE
I've never been so happy in my life. We both made a sacrifice and that's worth more than all the gold and precious jewels in the world. Just to know that you gave up a prized possession is proof enough that you love me.

JOHN
I've always loved you, Blanche. I may holler and rant and act like a first-class crumb sometimes—but you never doubted that I loved you, did you?

BLANCHE
No, John.

JOHN
It's been eight years, honey—most of it uphill. I haven't showered you with diamonds, or bought any yachts—but I try not to deny you anything. I suppose you have your little faults—what woman hasn't—or what man either, for that matter? We're both pretty sensitive people—maybe that's why we beef so much. Still, I don't think we're any worse than any other married couple. At least we have a safety valve and we can let off steam. Some of the others just carry it inside until the break comes. No, Blanche, I like it this way. And I love you more than anything on this earth.

BLANCHE
Oh, John.

JOHN
Hey, cut that out! I'll prove how much I love you. Where's that liver or rice pudding or whatever it is you made?

BLANCHE
It's liver.

JOHN
I'll eat every bit of it if it kills me!

They walk to the dresser and he start stuffing himself.

                    BLANCHE
          Merry Christmas, darling.

                  JOHN (mouth full)
          Merry Christmas, darling.

                                      FADE OUT

                  THE END

Hear the Shows...

Buy the Original,

Official Recordings At

www.bickersons.com

Available now at
http://www.bearmanormedia.com